WITHDRAWN

THE SHAMAN'S STONE

THE SHAMAN'S STONE

Hugh Scott

Andersen Press · London

To my wife
MARGO
for her loving support
as I learned to write.

First published in 1988 by
Andersen Press Limited,
62-65 Chandos Place,
London WC2

British Library Cataloguing in Publication Data
Scott, Hugh
The Shaman's stone.
I. Title
823'.914[F]   PR6069.C58/
ISBN 0-86264-195-0

0862 641   950   5538

Typesetting by Print Origination (NW) Ltd., Formby, Liverpool
Printed and bound in Great Britain
by Anchor Brendon Limited, Tiptree, Essex

Chapter 1

The moon was a cold eye in the sky's sullen face, and branches, bare as winter, made black lines on its brightness.

'I hate being here,' whispered Martha.

She pulled her nightdress up, clear of her knees, and knelt on the window seat. She tucked the nightdress over her feet and shivered a little in the darkness.

In the room behind her cooling embers made distant music, and shadows waited.

'This is the worst day of my life,' said Martha to the moon. 'I will write a story about today, and every child who reads it will cry herself to sleep for nights and nights and nights.'

The embers clinked loudly and Martha turned.

The shadows stood very still.

Martha faced the moon and wept as Mummy's voice echoed in her memory, 'Daddy's dead. Daddy's dead. Daddy's dead.'

Martha breathed deeply and kept the breath tight inside. Then she let it go.

'Come in, Mummy,' she said.

Beneath her lay the garden, rather grand and rather tangled, looking like a scattered treasure under the silvering moon.

She turned her face towards the door and said, 'Come in,' again. The ancient furniture groaned in its sleep. The oak door stayed shut.

Curiously, Martha undid her feet from her nightdress and crossed the room.

She opened the door.

'Mummy—'

There was no one on the landing. She went to the balustrade and peered over into the hall.

The lights were on. All the gleaming doors were closed. All the chairs sat back against the walls. Only the grandfather clock was awake, watching the time.

There was no one on the shadowed stair.

Martha went into her room and sat again at the window. Perhaps she'd heard a branch bumping on the house's wall. She wasn't familiar yet with the sounds of this house.

Cobwebs of cloud were shredding across the moon. The silver garden vanished into darkness and suddenly, all Martha could see was her reflection in the window, and teardrops of rain splashing on the glass.

'The story,' murmured Martha to her reflection, 'will tell of the move from our busy flat to the proud loneliness of the house with tall chimneys; of the wild garden without boundaries; of trees thickening into forests; of grass and wild flowers feeding on the land, leaving scarcely room for the roads that squeeze between the hillsides.'

Martha knew she was hiding from the dreadful thought that Daddy had gone. She had to fill her mind with words or she would scream until she was mad.

She went to her desk and sat on the cold leather chair. She fumbled for a pencil and stared at the blur of white in the darkness which was her writing pad. If she could write a poem—pour her sadness onto paper—she could ease the terror in her head.

Tears warmed her eyelids then spilled over and splashed on the leather desk-top. Her grief trembled inside her and filled her chest with heaving pressure which burst from her lips in a shuddering sob.

The knock sounded again.

Mummy's voice called gently, 'Martha?'

'Come in, Mummy.' Martha wiped her eyes with her sleeve and tried to steady her breath.

'Mummy,' she said, and let her mother's arms go round her. They sat together on the cold chair and wept.

Outside, the darkness wept with them, and the wind sobbed in sympathy with their tears.

'We must stop,' said Mummy. 'I'll make some cocoa.'

'I want to go back to the flat,' said Martha, but knew as she spoke, it was impossible.

The flat was sold. New voices moved within its walls; new sounds of living. Going back would not be the same as going home.

'It's all right,' said Martha at her mother's anxious glance. 'I didn't mean it.'

They went onto the landing.

'Did you knock before?' asked Martha.

'When?'

'A minute or two before you came in.'

'No—'

'I thought I heard you, and came out here.' Martha stared down. There were chairs as fat as old ladies, and chairs as thin as old men. They looked the same as last night when Daddy was still alive. Martha felt they should be different, maybe shouldn't exist, now Daddy was dead. It didn't seem right that silly things like chairs should go on, when something as important as a human being had gone.

'It's really quite grand,' said Martha.

They went down the shadowy stairs and into the hall's brightness. 'Did we pay a lot for this house?' There was a fireplace in the hall like a huge open mouth, with dusty logs stacked on the hearth.

'Yes—'

'Can I light the fire? We'll make the house lived in. I don't want to go back to the flat—not really. Daddy wanted us to be here. We'll fill it with *our* sounds, and everyone will know *we* belong here. Don't you think a house has to fit people—like a new coat? We'll make it fit us—'

'I'll get the cocoa!' whispered Mummy, and hurried towards the kitchen.

Martha followed, and found newspapers left over from unpacking.

She went to the library and lifted her father's lighter.

She stood very still. The only noise was the mourning of the weather, and the crackling of the newspaper under her arm. The library was warm and smelt of cigars.

Martha's eyes found the ashtray among the papers and books on Daddy's desk. A line of blue smoke threaded up from a squashed cigar butt. Daddy always did that; never quite crushed them out.

Martha started to reach—

She froze, still as winter.

She felt her eyes widen.

Daddy had been dead half a day—how could his cigar still burn?

Martha turned very slowly.

Bookshelves.

Armchairs.

Drum table.

Curtains.

Martha's heartbeat was suddenly loud.

She backed towards the door. The cold brass handle filled her palm.

'Martha?'

8

'Oh!'

'What is it?' said Mummy pushing the door open. 'You're white as a sheet. You shouldn't have come in here. We'll have cocoa in the kitchen . . . .'

Martha hardly heard.

'There's someone behind the curtain,' she said.

'What?'

The curtain didn't move.

'You must have heard the wind,' said Mummy. She walked to the curtains and thrust them apart. 'No one. Now, cocoa. Come on.'

She eased Martha through the hall and into the kitchen. She hadn't seen the smoke or noticed its smell.

Martha drank her cocoa, staring at nothing.

The burning cigar had gone to the back of her mind. Tears warmed her eyes again and she wept silently, over-flowing with emptiness.

She looked at her mother. Her white skin was shadowed with grief. Her black hair, short and curled, moved with her head as a hat moves, without swinging. Her hazel eyes looked inwards showing Martha dismay and bewilderment. Death was hard to understand.

Martha's hair swung full and soft around her cheeks. She had the same colouring as her mother but was still a shade too chubby. Mummy said she would grow out of it—and she knew—because she had been chubby once, turning lean when she had suddenly grown up, at fifteen.

'What—' said Mummy.

She cleared her throat and started again. 'What made you think someone was in the library?'

Martha said, 'I just thought.'

It was easier than explaining. Sometimes it was difficult to talk to a grown-up—even a nice one like Mummy. Sometimes it was simpler to say, 'I don't know' or 'I don't care' rather than get caught in explanations. Anyway, she had no explanation; that was the problem. Mummy had enough to worry her. Martha had to help, not add to troubles. 'I think I could sleep now,' said Martha.

'Go to bed. I'll be all right. No need to look at me as if I were a hundred. Goodnight, darling.'

Martha went into the hall. The chairs, fat and thin, slept; the grandfather clock still counted seconds in its deep tocky voice. It seemed to watch her from the corner of its eye as she looked at the closed library door. She could hear the wind as it screamed in despair and threw rain against the narrow hall windows.

She walked quickly towards the library, conscious of her bare feet on the cold wooden floor. She turned the handle, threw the door back and switched on the light all in a rush.

There was no cigar smell.

The dead butt lay cold in the ashtray. The curtains were open as Mummy had left them. The warmth had gone from the room.

Martha switched off the light and closed the door quietly. She didn't like unexplained things. They made her uncomfortable; unsafe. How could that cigar smoulder all day? Was it possible someone was in the house?

Martha listened.

The clock seemed to tick louder.

She tried to close her ears to its sound but it got persistently in the way of the silence, overwhelming even the voice of the wind.

She crossed the hall, and heart thudding, threw open the drawing room door and dashed on the light switch.

Nothing.

No one.

She did the same at the dining room and the lounge, her heart hammering, beating in her ears, making her forget the clock, making her sweat.

There was no one.

She looked in every room, then went to bed, right under the covers, pulling her gown over her freezing feet, and the quilt up past her sweating brow.

She remembered she hadn't cleaned her teeth, but she lay too long deciding whether to rise—and fell asleep.

Martha opened her eyes in darkness.

The wind had changed direction and howled and whistled down the chimney, stirring the dead embers, rustling them like whispering voices in the night.

Martha knew the sound.

She closed her eyes and felt her cheeks pulling down as she remembered about Daddy.

The wind shrieked suddenly, startling her fully awake. She could no longer hear the embers, and certainly could never sleep through the surging wind.

The wind too, was like a voice—a voice that never paused for breath, crying her name in a hollow whistling. Ma-a-artha! Ma-a-a-a-artha! Ma-a-a-a-a-artha!

'Go away!' she whispered.

Ma-a-aaartha!

'You're only the wind!'

'Martha!' said the wind sharply.

Her eyes opened wide and she jerked up staring. There was the merest wash of moonlight in the room. She could see nothing but shining edges of furniture.

'Who's there?' she whispered, her mouth dry. 'Mummy!' she said loudly. 'Is that you?'

Chills shuddered down her back. She kept staring as she pulled the quilt round her shoulders, holding it at her front. 'Mummy?' The ribs of the central heating radiator gleamed and vanished as moonlight streamed in then snapped off. For a moment, Martha could see nothing, then a giant stood at her door, and her heart pulsed coldly, until she saw it was her dressing-gown on the hook. Then the wind sighed and fled groaning, leaving Martha surrounded by silence and the watching furniture.

She knew she had heard a voice. She knew that Mummy was asleep by now, asleep in the next room beyond the thick old wall. She knew that Mummy lay amid dreams in a bed too big for one person, and whoever had called . . . .

The room was suddenly warm. Martha looked and listened so hard it seemed that her skin was as sensitive as her eyes and ears. A little smile found her lips and opened her mouth to the darkness. The warmth was not the warmth of temperature, but the warmth of love.

'Daddy?'

Tears of joy splashed her cheeks. His presence was all around, embracing her face, her hair, her shivering body. Then it slipped away, and she waited. She lay down, still huddled in the quilt. He wouldn't return tonight. 'Thank you for coming,' she whispered, and large tears slid backwards across her temples, wetting her ears, and she smiled at the silliness of it, and rolled out of bed, feet to the floor, nuzzling her face on the quilt.

Moonlight. Her writing pad lay square on the desk. She sat on the leather chair. The quilt was long enough to go under her feet. She could see the lines on the paper, and the golden lettering, VENUS, on her pencil. Stars winked on beside the moon, and clouds hung, dark emptinesses.

She began to write, not really thinking, just her feelings, her tears, her unbelievable joy, stumbling in words onto the moonlit paper. Then she sat, hardly seeing the tangled garden below, and the silvered trees marching motionless across the countryside; rather, feeling the bliss of knowing that Daddy was alive—not as he was, not tall and handsome, with that funny way of raising his eyebrows trying to look severe but always close to laughter; and always something in his hands, perhaps a cigar, very often a book, frequently an artefact dug out of the ground or borrowed from a museum; and he spent hours and days, measuring, drawing, washing things in chemicals to preserve from rust or rot. Then he would write. He wrote almost as much as Martha, but adult writing, facts and dates, calculations, deductions. Using words like PRE-ROMAN, BRONZE AGE, TELLURIC, THE BEAKER PEOPLE....

Martha closed her eyes. That was all gone. Daddy was dead. But his love was alive, and he had been here, letting her know that death was simply change.

She opened her eyes.

She didn't believe what she saw.

Something that walked like a man was pushing through the undergrowth in her garden.

Chapter 2

Martha fled towards the giant and with a snatch turned it into her dressing-gown, thrust her hands through the sleeves, and turned the brass doorhandle.

She glanced back. The quilt sprawled on her carpet like a great black slug, and skeletons of trees held thin fingers across the moon. She couldn't see down into the garden. She ran to Mummy's room, and pushed at the soft mound of her mother's body.

'Mummy!'

'Martha? What's wrong?'

'Look out of the window! Ssh!'

'Oh, Martha! I've just fallen asleep—'

'You must look!' screeched Martha in a whisper. And Mummy sighed and stepped towards the curtain.

'Be careful!'

'Oh Martha.' Mummy jerked open the curtains and moonlight dazzled them.

'What am I supposed to be looking at?' said Mummy, shivering. 'I hope you didn't wake me for an owl or a fox—' Martha dug her little fingers into her mother's wrist to silence her. She couldn't see it. She couldn't see the thing that walked like a man. From this window though, lay a view up the high meadow, white as cloth in the pale light, and at the top, the standing stones of Ruggens Dolmen.

The garden was a tangle of silver, and beyond the brittle outline of the plum trees the hothouse gleamed, dark and transparent. Then she saw it! She released Mummy's wrist and prodded the night with her finger.

'Where?' whispered Mummy.

'In front of the hothouse! Mummy look! Look! I can see through it!' And her mother's hand crushed her shoulder, and they stood in terror, as the thing turned its face to the house, opened its jaws and howled dismally.

It was the cry of an animal lost in the fog; a cry from a dream; a cry, thought Martha, ringing through centuries of loneliness and savage longing. And as they stared, the jaws closed, it sniffed the night air, and dissolved into moonlight and darkness.

Mummy said, 'There!' and on the white slope of the meadow Martha saw movement, like the shadow of a dog rippling over the ploughed land, racing towards the dolmen. Then it was gone.

Martha suddenly wished she had lit the fire in the hall.

Mummy said, 'I could do with a large gin.'

'Should we put the lights on?'

'Why not!' cried Mummy. 'I don't believe this,' she said, half to herself. 'We weren't dreaming? Werewolves! We weren't asleep?'

'No,' said Martha. Mummy pulled on her dressing-gown and found her slippers with her toes. Martha seldom wore slippers. She enjoyed the soft roughness of carpets and the sudden chills of wood or stone.

They walked downstairs, switching on lights. The fat and thin chairs didn't stir, but the grandfather clock moaned and struck quarter to seven.

'I've slept longer than I thought,' said Mummy.

'I'm going to light the fire!' declared Martha.

'And I'm going to make us a proper breakfast for once!' announced Mummy, and she went to clatter in the kitchen while Martha found newspaper, and kneeling in the hearth of the hall fireplace, separated the pages, rolled them into tubes and bent them into large knots. Daddy had taught her this. She pushed the knots into the iron nest of the fireplace then piled on thin sticks for kindling. Matches were on the mantelpiece. She lit the newspaper, watching until the sticks were aflame, then stacked on logs from the pile in the hearth.

She sat on the rug, wondering at the beauty of the fire; wondering why she could take such delight in setting the paper and sticks just so, and feel suddenly happy, boisterously happy; then Mummy was singing, with scatterings of words and many la-las, an Irish air, from her childhood.

She uncurled her legs and padded to the kitchen.

'Why are we happy?' she said, and Mummy looked up from the business of pushing eggs and bacon around the hot frying pan.

'Have you lit the fire?'

Martha nodded a single nod.

'We can't be unhappy all the time,' sighed Mummy.

'It was only yesterday—'

'I know.' Two tears appeared among Mummy's lashes and rolled down her cheeks. 'Don't talk about it—'

'But, Mummy, I want to know *why* we are happy! Why? When Daddy is dead and strange things—'

'Smell that bacon! Wash your hands, Martha. Oh, I need a hankie!' Mummy blew her nose and dabbed her wet cheeks with her cuff. 'Why d'you ask such impossible questions? Sit down. Oops! There goes the toast!' And she puffed heartily into the toaster and presented Martha with two charred rectangles. She laughed, lips red around white teeth. Martha smiled. The blackened bread reminded her of the white square in the moonlight that was her writing pad.

'I wrote a poem,' she said and half rose.

'It'll keep,' said Mummy. 'Eat.' And Martha ate.

Mummy scraped the blackness off the toast and they crunched, and drank tea.

The electric light was fading as the sky paled. 'I'll get the poem.'

Martha sucked her marmalady fingers as she crossed the hall. She placed two more logs on the fire, pushing them so they couldn't fall forward. She switched out the light, but the slit windows were pale and cold, and she clicked the switch on again.

She took cool steps on the oak floor, towards the staircase.

She stopped on the first step, her toes curling into the carpet. Something was going to happen. She turned and faced the front door. Stained glass. Little protection. Her heart beat too fast. The grandfather clock tick-tocked in its old-fashioned voice.

She gasped. A human shape crept up the glass, and a nose and cheek in green and red squashed against Victorian roses, and an eye swivelled, looking in, searching the electrically lit hall.

Chapter 3

The palm of a large hand struck the glass.

'Anybody there?'

Martha panted with relief. A normal human voice.

'Are you people all right?'

Mummy came into the hall. 'Why aren't you answering the door?' she hissed, and she opened it the width of her face. Cold morning air swept under the legs of the chairs and the fire growled, its flames trying to escape up the chimney.

'I say! Are you all right? Sorry to trouble you—Down, sir!' Martha heard claws on the doorstep, and panting.

'Come in!' cried Mummy, swinging the door wide, then shutting out the wind.

'Hope you don't mind the dog! He's big but harmless. Aren't you, old chap? Shake hands with Mrs Lawson, Angus.' And Mummy, self-consciously fidgeting with her dressing-gown, caught the alsatian's raised paw. 'And who's this, eh?' Blue eyes twinkled at Martha. 'Come and meet him then.' And she ran across the rug and embraced the dog, dropping to her knees, and the great paws thumped her shoulders and a wet tongue warmed her ear.

'Isn't he marvellous!' cried Martha. 'He's so black and fierce-looking! Oh, Mummy!' and she thrust her hands into the thick fur, rubbing the muscled body vigorously. The black and brown tail swept the floor.

'By gum! You two are pals! I say—' He was noticing Martha and Mummy's dressing-gowns. '—I hope I didn't get y'out of bed. The lights were on. Thought you were up!'

'We were up!' said Martha, hugging the alsatian's neck.

'Come into the kitchen,' said Mummy.

'Oh. Call me Jeff. Short for Jefferson. Jefferson Wilson. Can never make up m'mind if it's a grand name or just plain silly.' And Jeff chose the sturdiest chair at the kitchen table and eased into it. Martha thought he was like Angus, with his strong head and neck and thick shoulders, but lean nearer the tail. Martha smiled at her thoughts, and Jeff grinned back. Forty, decided Martha, and nice. Not as nice as Daddy. She normally disliked ginger hair and moustaches, but she forgave Jefferson Wilson, because his ginger hair was soft and his moustache so fluffy that it leapt as he spoke in his puffy way, and his blue eyes were rascally good-humoured.

'I won't say no, Mrs Lawson,' cried Jeff as Mummy offered the teapot. 'Jill. Jill and Martha. I say.' He looked at Mummy solemnly and whispered. 'Heard about your husband. Everyone's very sorry. Hardly moved in . . . .' His large head indicated the house.

'Thank you,' said Mummy.

'I thought I'd better see you were all right. Fact is—' He glanced at Martha and one softly ginger eyebrow went up as if beckoning her close. 'Fact is, I spotted a prowler. I'm in Horseshoe Cottage. Just through the wood. About three hundred metres. Dead straight path, y'know, all nicely cobbled. Devilish odd when y'first see it, but it's an old pack horse trail. Yes. Angus woke me, growling, hair like a giant bottle brush. Never knew him so touchy.'

'Did you see it?' asked Mummy tensely.

'It? Oh, the prowler. More or less. Moonlight was playing tricks though. Went through the trees, transparent as a ghost. Flickering. Moonlight and shadow. As if there was no substance to him.' Jefferson Wilson reached down and put his hand on the alsatian's great head. 'Looked a bit like

Angus,' he mumbled.

Martha blinked, taking her eyes from Jeff's fluffy moustache. Mummy's gaze moved from her cup, to the butter, to the salt. Silence waited in the kitchen.

Jeff spoke again, quietly. 'I didn't hear anyone saying I'm silly.'

'We saw it too.' Mummy's soft red mouth was solemn. The pale sky brightened from grey to blue.

'It's going to be cold,' said Jeff. He sighed, making his moustache fluff. 'I don't believe in werewolves,' he said. No one answered, for neither Mummy nor Martha believed either, yet they knew. Angus sighed, like a slow echo of his master.

'Who is " everyone"?' asked Mummy. 'You said everyone was sorry about Grant.'

'Oh. Well. There's me, of course.' He frowned good-humouredly as if he couldn't think further. 'And Mrs Landsakes.'

'Mrs Landsakes?'

'Mrs McCorkindale, really, but I call her "Mrs Landsakes". You'll know why when you meet her. She's Scotch, like Angus.'

The dog's tail plopped once against the floor.

'A-and Mr McCorkindale.' Jeff lifted the teapot but it waggled emptily in his hand. Mummy took it and began making more tea. 'They live in the cottage next to mine. Retired postman, he is. Bad legs. Hardly goes beyond the garden. Then there's the vicar . . . .'

'He gave us the news about my husband,' said Mummy loudly.

Martha's chest suddenly wanted to burst with tears. She pushed back from the table and ran up to her room. All the sorrow about Daddy, all the fear of the night, made her weep, face down on her bed; and as she wept part of her mind stood aside, watching, like a kindly adult. And she was comforted. The shuddering breath steadied. Tears stopped. She rubbed her face in the pillow. Her quilt crouched on the floor by her desk. She sat up and pulled it onto the bed, over her knees. She noticed the pad on the desk and remembered her poem. She pushed the quilt away, and lifted the pad. She couldn't remember what she'd written, and her eyes were too blurred with tears to read the pencilled scrawl. Which was strange; her writing was usually neat.

She took the pad with her to the bathroom, washed her face, and went down to the hall. She switched off the light and stood on the rug blinking at the fire. On the mantelpiece was a tumbled row of books. Daddy's books, not yet in the library. And two or three stones in plastic bags which Martha knew were recent in Daddy's collection.

She glanced away and stared at her pad trying not to think about Daddy. Then blood fled through her, like freezing water. She stared, her eyes clear now, at the page of writing.

She began to scream.

Chapter 4

It was too much. Too much that she couldn't understand. The screams rushed out of her, emptying the energy that threatened to burst her mind. She closed her eyes, putting darkness between her and the world, and her own rending voice was all the sound she heard until Mummy's firm arms wrapped around her, and she hung in that safe grasp, letting the screams become moans, the moans, gasps. She rested her cheek on Mummy's breast. The pad dropped from her fingers. Something wet and friendly licked her palm. Jeff said something about a doctor and Martha gasped, 'No!' for though she was in despair, that kindly bit of her mind told her she was really all right.

'I think she's all right,' said Mummy. 'I'll put her to bed. Please put the kettle on, Jeff, and I'll fill a hot water bottle.'

And Martha lay under the quilt, tight in her dressing-gown, shivering, toes tapping the hot water bottle, the writing pad bright in her memory. It couldn't be true. It just couldn't be true.

Electric light was bright on her eyelids. She woke slowly, and saw the fire was lit, a small mountain of coal red-hot behind the fireguard. Curtains shut. Had she slept all day? Martha felt calm and refreshed. She would write. Perhaps just a description of her room. Something clever. The oldest piece of furniture was newest; the newest, oldest. Something like that. The antique desk was new to her, unlaced from cobwebs in the attic. A davenport, Daddy had called it when he carried it down. She had washed it with washing-up liquid and polished till her elbows ached. She loved its

22

ink-stained leather, sloping conveniently, and the rail around the top to keep pens from rolling over the back; like the wall beside the lawn. Lilliputian pillars of wood. She'd use that in her next book. And her old dressing table was modern; small in this room with its tall walls and ceiling crusted with plaster roses. It had been just right in the flat. But Daddy wanted to be here, to have space for his collections, peace to study; and it was easier to reach archaeological sites, instead of burrowing through traffic to escape London.

She heard Mummy's voice. Surely Jeff couldn't still be here! Mummy came in cautiously.

'You're awake. Do you feel better? I've brought someone to see you.'

'What's the time?' whispered Martha.

'About six. You didn't stir all day.'

'Is it Jeff?'

Mummy nodded.

'Still here?'

Mummy shook her head. 'He's been at work. And someone else . . . .' She opened the door.

Jeff tip-toed in, massive but graceful, bigger than the giant on the doorhook. Someone behind him. Taller than Mummy, same tapered strength as Jeff, same hair and blue eyes.

'Micky,' said Jeff. 'One third of my household.' The other third ambled to the bed, grinned at Martha, then sprawled at the fire, flapping his tail.

Micky smiled. One of his teeth was crooked, but it was a good tough smile with the ghost of a ginger moustache. He was about sixteen, thought Martha; she liked him instantly.

Micky strode in and sat on the quilt. 'You don't look ill,'

23

he declared, frowning like a doctor. His cold fingers pressed Martha's wrist, and he consulted his watch. 'Nothing wrong there. Quarter to six.' His finger approached Martha's eye and she giggled as he tugged down one lower lid, then the other. 'Two pupils,' he muttered. 'Not enough to start a school but worth getting tickled for.' And to Martha's astonishment, his big hands reached for her ribs and tickled her, making her screech and squirm for ten delicious seconds of torture.

As she lay gasping Micky stood up and told Mummy, 'I'm sorry, Mrs Lawson, but your daughter won't live more than another sixty or seventy years—Gosh! I'm sorry—'

Mummy smiled widely, and put her fingers on Micky's arm. 'It's all right. We don't want to be treated like Roman glass. We won't break. Grant is dead, and strangely enough, we're getting used to it.' She said to Jeff, 'This boy of yours is doing us good already.' She sat in the warm dent Micky had made in the bed. 'Micky's staying with us—' In her hand was Martha's writing pad, closed. '—for a few days.'

Martha took the pad.

'Will that be all right?' asked Mummy.

Martha folded back the cover and stared at the pages of writing. 'Oh. Yes,' she said.

'In case the prowler comes back.'

Martha looked at her mother. She saw neat black curls, hazel eyes slightly red with crying, the soft mouth; behind that, she saw adult strength. Jeff and Micky stood at the fire, watching, both with hands in pockets, both solid and good-natured. Like twins, one too old, one too young.

'I wrote a poem,' said Martha. 'In the night. By moon-light.' She looked at the davenport where she had sat. Two strong heads turned slightly. 'Daddy came.' Her mother's brows moved slightly, seriously. 'Just his warmth. I think it was him in the library, Mummy,' said Martha quietly as her mother reached forward anxiously. 'His cigar was burning. That's why I thought someone was in the room. Remember? But I understand now.' Martha looked at Jeff and Micky, then back at her mother. 'Daddy is trying to talk to us.' She turned the pad and placed it in Mummy's hand.

Mummy looked down. 'This is Daddy's writing!' she whispered.

'It's my poem,' said Martha. 'I wrote it.'

'What's this about a cigar?' asked Jeff quietly.

'It was in Daddy's ashtray. In the library, last night. The last time Daddy was at his desk was the night before, then he went to the site yesterday, where . . . .'

'Y'mean he wasn't home all day?'

Martha shook her head, her hair swinging softly at her cheeks.

'She's kidding us,' said Micky, but when Martha looked at him his fair skin brightened to red. 'Sorry,' he said. 'But are you sure? Certain sure?'

Martha nodded steadily, hair dancing.

'It couldn't burn for a night and a day!' said Micky.

'I don't understand!' cried Mummy, and her face moved weepily. 'He's dead! Leave him alone!' And she bent her head, black curls towards Martha, tears patting gently onto the paper.

Jeff and Micky shuffled uncertainly, as Martha pulled her legs from the bedclothes, and embraced her mother.

'I say,' Micky mumbled at Jeff, 'we should push off and make a cup of tea—'

'We're not Roman glass!' shouted Martha.

'Don't,' sighed Mummy. 'I'm all right. Really. We must

read this.' She dabbed a tearstain with her finger. 'Grant's writing was so bad! He could do beautiful lettering!' she squeaked.

'I'll read it!' announced Martha, and frowned at the pad, avoiding Micky who was red again, because she had shouted. 'It's funny. It's almost my poem; and the writing's mine for the first two lines.

> *Blackest night*
> *Brightest moon.*

Then it's Daddy's writing but still the poem.

> *Deepest sorrow*
> *Highest stone.*

It shouldn't be "stone". It should be "bliss".

> *The dead are a step nearer heaven*
> *Stone danger.*

Then scribbling!'

'Let me see!' cried Micky.

'Wait! Oh! Something-something. What *is* that? Learn, fern, turn . . .*return*! Something-something *return*. Then my poem.

> *Death's kiss, the body's sleep*
> *Bright morning of something.*

Is it danger again?"

She let Micky take the pad and share it with Jeff, their two heads coming together like a man in a mirror.

'It should be, "Bright morning of the soul",' sighed Martha, and was startled as Mummy held her hands and smiled proudly, nodding.

'She's been published you know.'

'Yes, it's "danger",' said Micky.

'Published?' puffed Jeff, and his moustache jumped in surprise. 'A book?'

'Mm,' said Martha, trying not to beam.

'Maybe it's in your shop!' said Mummy. 'Jeff has the bookshop—'

'What publisher?' asked Jeff.

'Carlton Imprints.'

'Yes. I know them. What's the title?'

'I say!' said Micky grinning. 'You're a very small button to be in print.'

'She's clever,' said Mummy, and Martha pulled up her shoulders and giggled. 'Tell Jeff the title. He may have it in stock.'

'If I haven't, I'll soon get it!'

'*Charlotte Under the Hill.*'

'*Charlotte Under the Hill,*' said Jeff scowling so fiercely that Martha giggled again. 'By Martha Lawson! Of course! You're Martha Lawson! I've got blurb on you somewhere! We could have a signing session! I say! We'll make you famous!'

'The most famous Button in England!'

'I'm sorry I shouted,' said Martha.

'Who shouted?' said Micky, and he looked round quickly, peered down his jumper, lifted Martha's hair and searched her ear thoroughly. 'No one's shouting.' And he grinned, showing his crooked tooth, and Martha noticed his freckles.

'I'll get dressed now,' she said. 'You can leave Angus,' she told them and the alsatian, struggling a little as he rose, circled once, then lay down again.

Martha slipped off her dressing-gown and stood in her nightdress at the wardrobe mirror. She tidied her hair with

27

her fingers then found a hairbrush under the bed and began brushing. 'You're really quite old,' she said, and watched Angus in the mirror. 'What are you? Twelve? Same as me. Am I horribly fat? Daddy says "chubby".' She stopped brushing. 'My colour's better! In summer I turn brown, like Mummy. I think Mummy's beautiful. I wonder if Micky likes me. He tickled me. And touched my hair.' She went on brushing. 'My cheeks are fat.' She puffed them out, then brushed her hair forward over her face. She swept it into a middle parting and looked at her own brown eyes. 'I might be beautiful eventually. But fifteen is forever! Maybe I'll be slim before then. Do you know, Angus, that children mature more quickly nowadays? I learned that at school in London. I wonder what the school here is like? I don't suppose you know.' She smiled and looked for the dog in the mirror.

He was gone.

She saw the carpet, strangely empty in front of the fire. She turned.

The curtains were lifted at the bottom, the alsatian's black and brown rump supporting them.

'Angus.'

The tail moved.

'What are you looking at?' Martha began pulling on her clothes. Her fingers wouldn't move fast enough. She zipped her skirt. Popped her head through her jumper, and shook her hair into shape as she ran to the door. The brass light switch was hard in her palm. She took a breath and clicked the room into darkness. With firelight.

The fire ticked and rustled, wonderfully warm. The alsatian came from the shadows and looked up at her. Then he trotted back to the curtain, put his nose under it and lifted. Martha went with him. She crouched with the curtain on her shoulders and her arm across the dog's back.

She could see almost nothing. The moon wasn't up. She found a star deep in the night. The floor under her knees was hard and cold. She saw where the sky fell behind the trees, pale darkness beyond dead winter limbs.

Angus growled at her ear. The fur on his back stood up mysteriously around Martha's hand. She could see nothing. But she knew.

She knew.

Chapter 5

Something like a fingerprint touched the glass outside.

A snowflake. Martha hunched her shoulders and pulled her mouth into odd shapes. Another snowflake clung to the glass. She leaned a little into the cushion of the window seat. More snowflakes rushed at the window and looked in at her. She had lost the star. Angus's fur relaxed, and he backed from under her hand unhurriedly. Martha followed him to the fire and sat with her arm round his neck.

'What did you hear?' she whispered. 'Was it howling again? A cry too thin for my ears? And you saw something, before the snow pressed whitely on my window. Is it a poor demented beast, lost, somehow, in the present, longing for its past? Or is it a demon, a wretched, baleful creature, full of vile feelings—'

Martha stopped and breathed deeply. She was frightening herself. In the fire, coal dropped suddenly and she jumped and the alsatian jerked nervously.

'I think we'll go downstairs.' She went to the door and clicked the light switch. 'Come on,' she told Angus.

She waited until she'd found the switch for the landing and the hall below; the staircase really was grand with oak wainscotting higher than she could reach. It needed polishing. Then she snipped out the bedroom light. She went down the staircase with Angus warm against her leg. The hall fire was low, but the fireplace with its marvellous mouth of grey stone, and the rich Victorian woodwork, gleamed. Mummy was beginning to clean the house. 'Making it fit us,' thought Martha. She put two logs onto the embers. 'And I will use the library; sit at Daddy's desk until it is my

30

desk, and use the books until they are my books. He wanted so much to be here.'

She closed her eyes and forced her thoughts forwards until they were at her forehead. She spoke quietly. 'We'll make this lovely house our home, Daddy. We'll fill it with our sounds. Our voices will live in the corners. Our thoughts will vibrate in the stones, from the earth below this floor, to the tall chimneys . . . . And nothing fearful will drive us out. I know you can hear me, Daddy. And we have help, wonderful help, I think, in Jeff and Micky. Though we'd rather have you—'

Something scraped blood-curdlingly down the stained glass of the front door. She gasped. Angus bounded from her side. He barked wildly, and raised himself, standing as tall as a man, and something outside brushed the Victorian roses and vanished.

Jeff was first in the hall. 'Down, sir!' And Angus dropped, still barking. Micky quietened him, and Mummy ran to Martha, eyes dark with fear.

'It's that thing!' gasped Martha.

'Oh, is it?' said Jeff grimly, and opened the door. There was no wind to sweep among the chair legs, but flames on the new logs flickered uneasily, and the air chilled. 'Hold him,' ordered Jeff, and Micky held the alsatian's fur. 'It's snowing.' Jeff went down the steps, and Martha and Mummy waited behind Angus. Jeff stood in the light that leaned yellow from the doorway, and fat snowflakes fell, embracing the already white ground. Jeff faced the woods, then the lawn.

'I can't see a thing!'

'What are those marks?' Micky was pointing at the doorstep. 'Footprints?'

Martha saw narrow scuffs in the snow. They filled in as she watched, white and smooth. 'It scratched the glass,' she said, and they examined the door in the poor light, but found nothing.

'I wish I had my shotgun!' said Jeff. 'By gum! What are we standing here for? Where's my coat?' And he rushed past them towards the kitchen and re-appeared shrugging into an old sheepskin. He pressed bone buttons through buttonholes with one hand, and dug a torch from his pocket with the other. 'You stay here,' he told Micky. 'I'll take Angus!'

'Don't go!' cried Martha.

Jeff's eyebrows were firm above his blue eyes. He looked at Micky. 'Tell them,' he said, 'who the wrestling champ was, of eight R.A.F. camps.' He smiled suddenly and touched Mummy's hand. Then he was down the steps and searching the ground, the great dog at his side, and they walked out of the light, vanishing into darkness behind the white falling snow.

Micky said, 'Dad,' very softly, to himself.

'Let's go in,' said Mummy. 'He'll be back in a few minutes.'

Micky was still staring into the descending white night. 'I say!' he said and grabbed Martha by the shoulders. 'We'll put all the lights on! And open the curtains! That's all right, isn't it, Mrs Lawson? So he can see!'

'Yes—'

'Ground floor first!' And he dashed into the drawing room.

'Soup's nearly ready,' said Mummy to his back.

Martha went into the library, switching on lights, rattling curtains. Snowflakes dimpled black windows. On Daddy's desk, the ashtray was clean, the cover snug on his typewriter.

Books and papers were tidied. Mummy hadn't touched anything else. His gold pen, which he never took outside; his chunky silver pencil with 2B lead for sketching; his baby microscope, and a photograph of Stonehenge with Midsummer sunrise bursting between the sarsen stones.

Martha sat in the chair. She shivered and hunched her shoulders. There were two fireplaces with a window between. The curtains had left dust on her fingers. And the books in the bookshelves were dusty. Thousands of books all round the room, holding the thoughts of dead people, for the books were as old as the house. Daddy's books were still in cardboard boxes, neat rows on the carpet claiming to be tomato soup, fruit cocktail, fragile . . . .

Martha opened a drawer. Daddy's diary peeped out at her. She lifted it onto her lap and opened it.

'Definitely ill,' said Daddy's difficult writing. 'Not imagination—though if I breathe deeply I can appear all right, so Jill and Martha have noticed nothing. Terribly drained. Maybe just 'flu. If I don't feel better tomorrow, will consult a doctor. I wonder what he can do for dreams of Anubis. I think I am terrified.'

Terrified.

Terrified and ill. All Martha knew was that he had collapsed and been driven by Dr Bellamy to hospital straight from the stone circle at Rollright.

'Caught you!' said Micky, his ginger head grinning round the doorpost. He came in. 'I say, Button, you're not crying?'

Martha put her woolly forearm across her eyes to catch the tears. 'I didn't really notice,' she whispered. She laid the diary into the drawer. 'Is the soup ready?'

'Yes. Dad should be back in a jiffy. I say, have you ever been on a donkey at the seaside? Dad calls me a donkey!' He fell on his hands and knees and snorted.

'That's a horse!' cried Martha.

'Nay!' said the donkey, and Martha bumped down on the donkey's back and digging in her spurs was galloped through to the kitchen and into the hot smell of soup.

'Whoa!' said Mummy. 'Soup!'

'Fodder!' cried the donkey, and Martha slipped off him and sat at the table. She suddenly remembered that she'd slept all day. Now she was hungry.

Martha clattered her spoon into the empty plate. Mummy supped quietly, rescuing, with her bread, a strand of leek that dangled from her lip.

'He should be back,' said Micky.

The black panes of the kitchen window had gathered soft corners of snow. The door to the utility room was shut tight and in the utility room was the door to the back yard. Locked and bolted. Shutting out the night. Shutting out the fear they didn't understand.

Micky leaned over the sink, cupping his hands to the window.

'There's stew to follow,' said Mummy, 'and I've found a tin of peaches for after.'

'I'm going to look out the front,' said Micky.

Martha went with him. He stood in the dropping snow looking towards the woods, then towards the lawn. Like a smaller Jeff, thought Martha. She wondered how she would describe him in a story. A lion? She eased her soles off the chill step and stood on the edges of her feet. Lions were old-fashioned. He was the right colour, though. And brave. And Jeff was brave! She shivered at the thought of walking in the shrubbery, claws of bushes dragging her clothes, hunting the thing that walked like a man. Even with the mighty Angus

34

beside her, she would be sick with fear.

'Dad!' called Micky. 'Da-ad!' But only the silence answered and smothering snow attacked the ground.

Micky ran up the steps and swept Martha into the hall. 'Get me a torch, Button. Something's wrong out there!'

'Let go of me!' cried Martha, fear bristling inside her. 'You can't leave Mummy!' And she stepped away from him staring up at his startled eyes, seeing his soft moustache.

He came at her suddenly, and was on his knees and clasping her shoulders.

'My dad's *outside!*' he said urgently. 'You and your mum will be safe until I come back.'

Martha continued to stare. She knew he was right, but jabbing fear made her say unfair things. 'What happens if you don't come back?'

For a second blue eyes gazed at her, and she knew they recognised her terror. 'I'll go without a torch,' he said. And she cried as she ran to the utility room, ignoring the plates of stew that steamed on the cooker, and Mummy's 'Martha?'

The torch lived on a shelf beside the back door. She snatched it down, clicked it on and off and rushed it into Micky's grasp. He was zipping up an anorak. He looked tremendously strong. He put his large hand on Martha's head and she felt heat rushing from his palm through her scalp. His face was blurred by her tears.

'Thanks, Button.' He went out, shutting the glass door gently between Martha and the darkness.

She went to the kitchen and sat in front of her plate of stew.

'He's gone out?' asked Mummy.

Martha pulled her lips tight.

Mummy sat down with her food but didn't eat.

35

Two brass taps peered into the sink.

On the worktop was the peach can, its tattered lid angled up, its reflection hanging beyond the black and snowy glass.

Outside, something glinted.

Jeff's torch, perhaps, searching the garden. Or something closer?

Something small and close.

It moved, and looked at Martha.

A row of fangs appeared.

A second eye glared in, and a tongue spilled moistly, horribly, from among the fangs.

It wasn't Angus.

Chapter 6

An arm, dressed in sheepskin, came out of the night. It encircled the throat, below the hot mouth and the jaws snapped shut, open and shut, left right, black lips snarling, eyes flickering white rims, CRASH! Mummy and Martha screeched, Mummy turning, seeing for the first time the violence at her window. An elbow had smashed the glass, and feathers of snow flew into the warm kitchen.

'It's Jeff!' screamed Martha. And they heard Jeff grunting with effort and muttering into the furry head that bit the air so near his face. Froth fell from the lips and the teeth clicked as they shut on nothing, and deep lines grooved Jeff's cheeks as he strained to hold on.

'If he lets go, it'll kill him!' cried Mummy. 'Where's Angus? Angus!' she screamed. 'Angus!'

The black snout of the creature smeared an unbroken pane.

'Rope!' gasped Martha. 'Mummy, the clothes-line! Where is it? We can tie it up!' And Mummy ran to the utility room. She flung open a cupboard beneath the sink. A bottle of bleach tumbled out and spilt on the floor.

'Oh! Here!' Mummy thrust the bundled rope at Martha and reached for the back door. She stood very still, panting through her red lips. Her throat moved as she swallowed.

'Mummy!' squealed Martha. 'You must!'

Her mother's hazel eyes glanced at Martha, not seeing her. But she pulled back the top bolt, turned the key and jerked the door fiercely. Snow. Softly descending. Mummy snatched the rope and pushed Martha violently, sending her staggering backwards into the kitchen; and Martha stopped herself against the table. The door slammed, shutting her in safely. Then to her astonishment she saw through the window a loop of white rope and her mother's small hands. And the beast snarled frantically as the rope curved over its head and tightened deep into the fur. Then a single bark cracked like a gunshot above the snarling, and Angus was there, fantastically wild, unbelievably savage. And suddenly, it was over. Blood drained cold down Martha's back. It was over, but no victory. She had stared hard, for it seemed that snowflakes were falling unhindered by the terrible gnashing head; dropping through it as if it were a hologram projected emptily into the night air. Then it was gone. Just Jeff panting, leaning against the window-sill, and Mummy crying, 'Oh!' with each breath, and Micky's voice desperately anxious.

Martha fled to the back door and rushed into the snow in her stockinged feet. Jeff eased himself off the window-sill, still panting. Mummy was holding the loop of rope, staring at it as if doubting its reality. Angus was lumbering here and there, sniffing the white ground, searching the air with his nose.

Micky put an arm round Mummy and another round his father. He brought them towards the door. They sat bewildered at the table. Mummy clattered the rope down onto her cutlery, shaking her head.

'Now we know what we're up against!' gasped Jeff.

'Martha!' said Mummy. 'There are bottles and glasses in the drawing room. Please, darling.'

Martha walked, shoulders hunched. In the hall she pulled off her socks which were wet from the snow, and spread them on the hearth. She went into the drawing room, leaving the polished door open behind her. The light was on, showing fat snowflakes dropping past the windows. She was curiously calm. She imagined herself as a waitress as she put bottles and glasses on the best silver tray, but a part of her mind that had no pictures in it, but only whispers of words, wondered at how calm she was, and remembered how happy she'd been after seeing the thing that walked like a man, the first time.

She lifted the tray, balancing it carefully. Mummy had been happy too, singing, with her Irish accent showing just a little. The bottles slid. Martha put the tray down quickly, and changed her grip. Above the sideboard hung a mirror in an ancient gold frame. Oak leaves and acorns wrestled with bryony, chipped slightly showing the plaster beneath the gold leaf. She saw herself and the room behind her. Her hair was untidy, and her cheeks too pale. She suddenly wanted summertime to burst into her life, so she could turn brown under the sun and leave sorrow in the past.

She glimpsed Micky in the doorway. Then she couldn't see him for her own reflection. She saw the best furniture. The wood-panelled walls and ceiling. Daddy's favourite painting of sailing ships, by a Dutch artist whose name she couldn't pronounce and therefore couldn't remember. She lifted the tray again and turned round.

Chapter 7

'Oh, God!' whispered Martha, and her words were a prayer ripped from her soul, for it wasn't Micky she'd glimpsed in the mirror, but the terrible thing that stood tall as a man. It wasn't solid. Behind it in the hall, one of the fat padded chairs that reminded Martha of an old lady in blue, cast a dark shadow. Martha could see the shadow through the creature's leg. She stared, trying to make sense of its vague solidity. Was it a man's body or a wolf's? Or some strange blending of both? And the head, clearly a wolf's head, tilted, like a dog waiting a command.

Martha's muscles in her neck went rigid like wood. She wanted to drop the tray to attract help from Jeff, but her brain couldn't unlock her fingers. The thing stepped forward and the jaws opened, then it faded, leaving the chair perfectly visible. And suddenly the room was warm and smelled of roses, reminding Martha of Daddy and a garden in the Isle of Man packed pink with blooms that scented the air all the way to the beach.

Daddy was here! Immediately, Martha was fiercely happy. She marched forward, breathing the perfume. Straight through to the kitchen.

On the brass taps at the sink snow was melting. Behind them, the bread board blocked the shattered window.

Jeff grabbed the tray and glugged whisky into glasses and gin for Mummy. 'I can have a sherry,' said Martha calmly. 'I brought it specially.' Mummy nodded. 'And I'm starving.'

'Why are you so cheerful?' demanded Micky pulling his chair close to hers and digging into his stew.

'We noticed this before, didn't we, Mummy? After we saw that thing the very first time. Mummy was singing . . . .' Martha relaxed her fork onto the plate. She was remembering her feelings then; her feelings now. 'I was terrified,' she whispered. 'Then when it was over, I was floating, excited. It's like coming out of the dentist's. As if something that usually anchors me to ordinary things is cut, and I rush upwards, a free spirit . . . .' She noticed Jeff staring.

'No wonder she writes!' gasped Micky at her ear.

'Hm!' said Jeff, and his eyebrow beckoned, but he said nothing.

'It was in the drawing room,' said Martha quietly. She went on speaking without looking up, feeding herself small forkfuls of meat. 'But it was thin like a ghost and faded away. Daddy came. Just his love, like last time, and the scent of roses. Remember the Isle of Man, Mummy? And the garden? And Daddy trying to catch a fish? I don't want to cry! I'm too hungry to cry!' And she snatched a mouthful of sherry and scalded her throat with its sweet cold sting; and she gasped and stayed calm.

They ate peaches and Micky sealed the smashed window with sticky tape and a square of soft plastic cut from a bin bag.

'So it was in the house,' sighed Jeff grimly. His moustache was wet with coffee. 'We went into the trees,' he said softly. 'Angus and me. We came across its footprints. Narrow scores like on the doorstep. Didn't realise what they were, until Angus bristled. But we lost them. Went through a thicket too tight for a rabbit. Thing must've been insubstantial when it went in. Comes and goes like a bad dream. We circled the house. Then Angus took off—'

'He came to me,' muttered Micky.

41

'—then I saw the marks again. All the house lights were on, and snow streaming down. And the beast stood outlined at the kitchen window. Thought it was Angus, but it was the wrong shape. Long legs for walkin' upright, and broader shoulders than any dog. Now it can get into the house.' His blue eyes looked at Martha sadly, then at Mummy. 'How can I protect you?' he whispered. 'That thing is stronger than I am! How do we fight it?'

Martha pulled her mouth very tight. She refused to be panicked. She gulped her coffee and broke a biscuit with her lips. Snowflakes rushed against the windowpanes and slid, building triangles of white. The square of black plastic bulged as the wind leaned on the house.

'You can't stay here,' said Jeff suddenly.

Mummy's dark curls moved as she looked at him.

He said, 'You must come with us. Spare beds upstairs under the roof. Cosy, y'know! I can't protect you here!'

'Can you protect us there?' asked Mummy.

'I'm hoping it won't come.'

Mummy sat back in the kitchen chair, tears in her lashes, mouth soft, ready to cry.

'You're probably right! And it's only just after seven o'clock! We seem to have lived a lifetime in this last hour!' Her Irish accent slipped among her words. 'I think we'll come! Martha? An evening of television? Just to relax, my darling?'

Martha tensed her shoulders, and gritted her teeth. She hated to be chased from her own home. But she had promised herself, in her heart, to help Mummy, and not add in the tiniest way to her sorrow. She nodded, hiding her face in her dark hanging hair.

'It's welly weather!' said Mummy brightly.

'My socks are in the hall!' said Martha, and she ran, cool-footed on the oak floor, roughly warm on the rug. Her socks were dry enough, and she sat on the rug with the fire hot on her legs as she pulled them on. She looked at the drawing room door, still open, and the electric light shining on its polished panels. When she had written *Charlotte Under the Hill* she had wondered just how scary it would really be in a haunted house. The reality terrified her. And yet—she frowned at the thin and fat chairs; the grandfather clock with its pendulum heart swinging tick-tock behind its glass front; and yet, where was fear? Behind the glittering doors? Tick-tocking in the pendulum? Waiting on the stairs? Even as Martha asked herself, she knew. Fear was nowhere. 'There is no fear,' she told the narrow windows, 'unless I create it.'

Then she went from room to room pulling curtains, switching out lights. In her own room she put tights on under her damp socks, then gathered night clothes and toothbrushes.

In the kitchen, the smell of bleach was strong. Mummy was pulling off rubber gloves. 'I don't suppose the utility floor's ever been so clean,' she said. 'Here are your things.' And Martha stepped into her wellingtons and Micky hoisted her anorak up her arms, hood over her head.

She pushed the hood back. Angus's wet nose touched her knee, then found her palm. She scratched his head.

Mummy made sure her key was in her handbag, then pulled the door closed. Martha stood in the snow, watching the thick feathers sway around her as the wind commanded their dance.

Mummy took a deep breath. 'I've left the hall light on,' she recited to herself. 'Back door's locked. Cooker's off.

43

Toothbrushes. Martha, did you put up the fireguards? The one in your bedroom? Right.'

They hurried out of the garden where it merged with the wood. White knobs of snow on ancient fence posts were the only sign of a boundary. The two torches showed little white drifts among tree roots, and the trees waved black shadows at them in the swinging light.

Martha saw a glow beyond tumbling flakes. 'Is that your cottage?' But as she spoke she knew the light was too high and too near.

'It's a lamp-post,' said Micky.

'Among the trees?' cried Mummy.

'It's really for your benefit, Jill,' said Jeff. 'Your house being where it is. Sort of last straggler outside the village. The next lamp-post is between Mrs Landsakes and me. See it in a jiffy.'

As they approached the light, the snow became more confusing, turmoiling as the wind twisted through the wood. When she looked up at the bulb, Martha saw the snowflakes as a rushing globe of white particles. Then she was past, watching for the next lamp-post.

Quite suddenly, the wind was silent. Micky, his big hand securely under Martha's elbow, had the top of his head towards the snowflakes. Mummy's face was at Jeff's shoulder, and Jeff looked constantly into the trees.

Cold spiders crept on Martha's back.

How could the wind be silent?

She stopped walking, making Micky stop. 'Mummy!' she said. And they stood still, each realising the strangeness, as they surfaced from their thoughts.

They stepped closer to each other, four people amid ghostly rushing silence. Tree limbs moved a little, and shadows slid cunningly from the torchlight, but it was like a film with sound shut off. Behind them the light from the lamp-post flickered among swirling feathers, then vanished.

'But it's not dark!' hissed Martha.

Micky's arm went round her shoulders. He switched off the torch with a loud *click*. Jeff's torch went out.

Unearthly.

It was the only word. Martha could see the trees. The light grew and the snow particles darkened.

Then something moved.

Among the trees, something moved.

Chapter 8

Men and women.

The dawn ripened. Children wrapped in fur. Adults in neatly-sewn fur garments, walking between primitive houses. Carrying earthenware pots, shouldering baskets. Circular houses clad with turf; some thatched. Smoke touching the sky.

One man sang without sound, sitting, his head rolling, eyes half closed. His arms and face were brightly marked with rings of blue and yellow. His mouth stopped singing. Four men carried a cage and placed it before the singer. In the cage was a wolf. The singer stood and drew from his clothing a short wand. Starting at a corner of the cage he cut a line in the earth, curving away from the cage, then returning. Almost a circle. The wooden gate was lifted and the wolf stepped out. The four men carried the cage away and the singer completed the circle behind the wolf.

Men, women and children watched. The men held axes. In the middle of the circle was a stone with rings carved into it. And the wolf paced, round and round, unable, it seemed, to cross the line in the earth.

Then the singer sat, and his mouth spoke. His eyelids quivered. Men gathered, enclosing the circle. Arms rose and fell, then they moved away carrying something.

The stone in the circle was red. The wolf was gone. The singer stood up, looked at the stone for a moment then raised his arms triumphantly. It began to rain.

Like cold kisses on Martha's face. Snow cluttered her eyelashes, and when she blinked, the only light was the glow from the lamp-post, and the trees were black lines in a black void.

The torches made bright cones of twisting flakes, and they stepped into the cones, following the path towards the next lamp-post, whispering so the dark couldn't hear.

Martha glimpsed a thatched roof with two windows hooded in snow, and a chimney towering into the night, breathing a ghost of smoke. In the garden rows of little green skeletons wore white shrouds. She would have guessed, she thought, that someone strong lived here, for heavy things like the garden roller and thick logs for the fires, were firmly in their place, not half-put-away by feeble arms, and the front door was solid, and closed sharply behind them as if it knew its duty.

Angus blurred into a fuzzy barrel as he shook off snow. They hooked their outdoor clothes on an old-fashioned hallstand and left wellingtons in a tumble on the carpet.

'Upstairs,' said Jeff. 'Two bedrooms. Take the one on the left. Loo's downstairs, I'm afraid, but y'can wash up there.'

So they went up, Mummy's slippered feet and little ankles turning steeply towards the roof; fumbling for a light switch, ducking into the tiny timbered doorway, saying, 'Ooh!' with approval as flowered walls closed around them in welcome, and the ceiling leaned down for a better look. The bed sparkled brassily and was fat with quilts. Martha clambered into the window space and gazed down on the garden. Their footprints were already white; the lamp-post a hanging sphere of snowflakes.

'It's lovely!' she said.

'We've a washhand basin,' said Mummy, gushing the tap. 'Where are the toothbrushes?'

'Plenty of books!' said Martha, noticing paperbacks on a neat shelf beside the bed.

'We're only staying the night!'

'I know.' Martha plunged onto the bed and rolled over. 'It's so soft!'

'Toothbrushes.'

'On the hallstand, I think. And so cosy!' She relaxed. 'What's happening to us, Mummy?'

'I don't know.' Her mother sighed, and sat on the bed. Her hazel eyes were warm. 'Are you very frightened?'

Martha shook her head until her hair criss-crossed her face, and she giggled.

'If Daddy's with us,' said Mummy, 'we don't need to be frightened.'

'He is with us.' Martha sat up. 'That cigar was actually burning. Blue smoke, real as could be! Daddy was there!'

Mummy's finger slid cool on Martha's brow, parting her hair, looping it back from her face. 'You're like your daddy,' she murmured.

'Four foot ten and chubby.' And they laughed at the unexpected humour.

'That's why people climb mountains, I suppose,' said Martha. 'And commit crimes. Haven't we had terrific bursts of happiness? Do you think, Mummy, that people aren't really awake? What if all our life is a dream, and only sometimes—like when we are afraid—we wake up properly, and really see things and really know things?'

'Well I hope you don't take to a life of crime. Or even mountaineering. Let's go down.'

The living room windows were snugly curtained, imprisoning heat from the iron stove in the fireplace. The stove's glass doors stood wide and fresh coal nestled in flames.

'Burns day and night,' said Jeff from the kitchen. He peered at them under the lintel. 'I'm making cocoa. That

48

all right?'

'*I'm* making cocoa,' called Micky.

'Lovely!' said Mummy.

The floor dipped and bumped, beautifully uneven, and layers of rugs were luxurious under Martha's stockinged feet. The big desk had a crushed milk carton under one corner holding it level; and the sideboard, crowded with pot plants and burping wine jars, sloped as if sinking under the load. Thick-framed water-colours hung at angles on the lumpy walls—pictures of grassy clumps with flowers and toadstools. Just above Martha's reach an oak beam sagged beneath the weight of two bedrooms and a thatched roof. 'And ever-thickening snow,' added Martha. 'I wonder if the night, crammed with stars, presses down, making the oak creak after sunset.'

Angus rolled in, licking his lips, smelling of dog food. He swung his tail at Mummy, then at Martha and sat at the television.

'Cocoa up!' said Micky. 'Not just now, Angus. He likes nature programmes.'

Jeff ducked in from the kitchen and rummaged under the sideboard. He grinned at Mummy and plopped brandy into her cocoa. 'Knocks you out if you're not used to it,' he said kindly, and Mummy smiled up at him.

Jeff settled in his armchair and he and Micky talked with Mummy, discussing what they had seen among the trees.

Martha's cocoa lay hot and milky on her tongue. It drained into beautiful patterns on the inside of her mug. She made it last by counting to ten between each sip.

Jeff had a book in his hand. 'Automatic writing,' he was saying quietly, 'is communication from the dead.'

'You mean Martha's poem,' said Mummy. 'Anything

49

else?' And her smile was too bright.

'Um . . . .' Jeff flicked the pages. 'Oh, here we are. Shamans. They were magicians. Even 'way back in Neolithic times. Here's a photograph of a Red Indian shaman. What we saw, I think, was a Stone Age or Iron Age ritual. Not ghosts—least I shouldn't imagine. More a natural recording, like a video-tape.' He sighed. 'Though what switched it on . . . .'

Silence grew, pressing emptily into Martha's ears. Then she heard the flames in the stove buffeting like clothes on a washing line. Micky's sleeve whispered as he lifted his mug. Somebody's tummy rumbled, and Martha giggled. Jeff's eyebrows went up and Mummy laughed gently.

'It was her,' said Micky, wagging his large finger at Martha.

'No it wasn't!' she squealed, and she let her hand drag through Angus's fur as he passed, walking to the kitchen.

'I confess!' cried Micky. 'That it was Angus!' And their laughter froze, as, in the kitchen, the great dog began to bark.

Chapter 9

Jeff jumped, then was up, pausing in the kitchen doorway to silence Angus with a whispered, 'Quiet, sir!' And Micky beside him was an echo, thought Martha, in her eye, rather than in her ear.

'It's all right,' said Micky. 'He's wagging his tail.'

Martha relaxed. Mummy's face was white, but glowed suddenly with a little smile.

Martha heard the outer door open and close, and a shrill Scots accent declared, 'Landsakes! Three of you to let me in! Who were you expecting in this weather? I don't suppose the Queen will be along again today. Get down, y'great daft lump!'

She waddled through pulling off her hat, which released springs of white hair. She used the hat to batter Angus, crying, 'I've nothing in my pocket!' but when she had flung her coat aside, there was something in her hand, and for ten minutes Angus nuzzled her fingers and was well rewarded.

Mummy's smile increased to a grin as Mrs McCorkindale put a hundred questions, and answered a thousand no one had asked.

At last there was silence.

Jeff shovelled coal into the stove.

It seemed to Martha, the old lady had something to say. Angus ceased searching her hand, and sprawled solidly on the floor.

'Donald's not well,' she said.

'Should I go through?' offered Jeff.

'No. No, he's got his pipe and the telly.'

'What's wrong with him, Mrs McCorkindale?'

asked Micky.

'He's an old fool.' Her voice was low and anxious. 'I don't know what came over him. Fidget! Fidget! "What's the matter?" I said. He said he had to dig up that sycamore. In this weather! I told him it had been there four years and could perfectly well wait till spring—but he did it. I thought you could stop him, Jeff, but you weren't in. Then he was so long that I followed him, and he was just standing in the snow, freezing, and with those legs of his. I put him to bed. He's got the telly. There's a bruise this length, up his forearm. He lifted a stone he says, and it was like touching a live wire. He was dreaming about cavemen when I brought him in—'

'Cavemen!' cried Micky.

And they all talked until the old lady was bewildered.

Stone.

Heat from the stove warmed Martha's brow and she sat back out of the conversation.

Daddy had mentioned stone. Mr McCorkindale, it seemed, had dug up a stone from under the roots of the sycamore. Then he had touched it. He had touched it just when Martha and Mummy, Micky and Jeff were walking in the snow on the pack horse trail. He had dreamed his dream when they had dreamed theirs. Touching that stone, thought Martha, had switched on what Jeff called 'a natural recording'.

She uncurled her legs and screwed her tights straight on her knees. She padded on the rugs and slipped between the curtains and the window, and peered towards the McCorkindales' garden. Her breath steamed the glass. She wiped a space, not breathing. She could see only Jeff's dustbin, close to the window, cosy-looking in its white woolly cap. And a glimmer of a greenhouse.

She recalled the hothouse in her own garden and the monstrous movement across moonlit glass. The memory shivered into goose bumps, and she stepped from behind the curtain into the room's heat.

Silence.

Wine plopped on the sideboard and she caught its sweet fruity fragrance.

Mummy, Micky and Jeff glanced at her, away from Mrs McCorkindale. The old lady's white curls jutted motionless. Her back moved as she breathed. Martha advanced curiously, then cautiously as Jeff's finger touched his moustache and Mummy's red lips opened in warning. What was happening?

She knelt beside Angus, fondling his chin, staring at the old lady.

Her nose stood out sharp between pendulous cheeks, and her lower lip dropped pink and moist. Her eyes were shut, but Martha sensed she wasn't asleep. A tenseness in her body suggested energy.

Martha was aware again of the oak beam and the weight of the night above her head and snow, flake by flake, quilting the thatch or hurrying to destruction against warm chimney pots.

Suddenly, she knew.

The warmth of love touched her, and when Mrs McCorkindale's mouth opened, Martha was only half-astonished to hear—not the voice of Mrs McCorkindale—but a man's voice, the voice of Grant Lawson, Martha's father.

Chapter 10

'Martha!' said Daddy. Mrs McCorkindale's old eyes looked down at Martha intelligently. 'Don't touch the dog! I'm using him too! Contact is weak. Is your mummy here?'

Martha nodded, stupefied, towards her mother, and Mrs McCorkindale turned and stood up. She stepped forward with a movement so familiar and manly.

'Jill!'

Tears fled over Mummy's cheeks and her red lips moved, silently.

'Jill.'

'I'm here! Grant?'

'There's little time. The old woman is weak. The stone. Oh, no! Not yet!'

The voice rose. 'The shaman's stone—'

Mrs McCorkindale staggered backwards into her seat. She drooped, eyes closed. Then her lids flickered up naturally. Angus sighed. Mrs McCorkindale said, 'My, but you're awful quiet.'

For a moment, Martha was amazed. Was it over? Her amazement boiled into fury. Finished so quickly? Daddy alive again and gone in a second! Why couldn't the old woman hold on! 'You let him go!' she whimpered. 'You let him go!' she screamed.

And she wept as Mrs McCorkindale cried, 'Landsakes! What's up? What's wrong with the lassie?'

'She's exhausted!' gasped Mummy, and Martha buried herself in her mother's embrace. 'She didn't mean to be rude, Mrs McCorkindale.' Then in a tiny voice said, 'Couldn't you have held on?' And she turned Martha round guiding her, hands on shoulders, into the little hall with the old-fashioned hallstand, up the black staircase, leaving silence and awkwardness with Micky, Jeff and the old lady who could be possessed by the dead.

Martha shook herself headfirst into her nightdress. She squatted suddenly on the quilts. 'I need to *go*,' she said, and a big smile broke through her tears.

Mummy was drying her face and smelt of toothpaste. She looked at Martha from behind handfuls of towel. 'It's downstairs.'

Martha nodded.

'No dressing-gown?'

Martha shook her head.

'Your anorak's in the hall. Slip it on and go through.'

'Come with me.'

They went down the dark tunnel of the stairs and lifted the anorak from the hallstand. It chilled Martha's skin. They went into the brightness of the sitting room with its smell of wine and carpets.

Mrs McCorkindale looked sympathetically at Martha.

'I'm sorry I was rude,' said Martha. 'I didn't mean it.'

Mrs McCorkindale's white nose pecked the air slowly. 'That's all right, dear. I understand.' But her smile was puzzled.

Micky winked carefully, as if to say, 'She doesn't know what happened.'

Jeff's moustache leapt as he murmured, 'It's that way.' And Mummy followed Martha to the kitchen where they found a door that bumped behind the kitchen door and a little cloakroom crowded with large shoes, and wellingtons tidied from the hall. Like invisible people queuing for the

55

toilet. A third door, its glass panels crusty with flowers, hid the bathroom. Linoleum sucked heat from Martha's bare soles. She shivered as she finished washing her hands. Two fat shaving brushes stood like miniature guardsmen, and an old-fashioned wooden bowl of shaving soap was frothed with bubbles, cold since morning.

She came out to voices in the kitchen. Iciness tangled her naked legs until Mrs Landsakes left, then the back door blocked the wind.

'Your turn for the dishes,' Jeff told Micky, and Micky groaned and collapsed, half-filling the kitchen floor with his heavy limbs. He died dramatically. Martha sat on his stomach bouncing a little until the corpse grabbed her ribs, leapt up and rushed her, feet clear of the carpets, all round the living room, avoiding a smiling Jeff and Mummy, then zoomed under the low lintel into the kitchen and collapsed again, gasping and twitching ridiculously.

'It would be less energetic,' panted the corpse, 'washing dishes.' And it stood up and grinned with its crooked tooth. Martha giggled, and rubbed the sole of her foot against her leg.

'You'd better go in to the heat,' said Micky. His thick fingers held a bottle of washing-up liquid, and Martha saw his tough mouth soften, and his blue eyes gaze moistly sad. 'This reminds me of my mum,' he said.

Martha pressed her lips together. She wiggled her cold toes. She didn't speak.

'She could have lived ages, y'know. Her heart wasn't too strong. Not like me and Dad. But, she collected things, clumps of weeds and toadstools and stones. These are her paintings.' His eyebrows sent Martha's thoughts to the thick-framed watercolours in the living room. 'But—' He bumped a blue basin into the sink and squirted in liquid. He jerked the tap, sending water crashing onto the basin's plastic bottom. Martha felt the spray hot on her face. Micky turned the water off. 'But she ran home. Lay on the bed and never woke up. She still had her coat on. Thorns caught in it.' Micky placed dishes in the water and sponged them clean. 'She shouldn't have been running, of course. No one wanted to know why. Not even Dad. You ever read Sherlock Holmes, Button? The great detective. I detect. I knew my mum had been running. Thorns in her coat. And she always left plants in this sink, and stones on the worktop, but there were none. I found them scattered in the wood beside her basket. She'd been chased.'

'Chased?'

'She'd left deep footprints. I tracked them back behind your house—'

'The high meadow?'

'The high meadow, Button. She must have been coming from Ruggens Dolmen. The meadow was ploughed up so there were no plants except around the standing stones.' Micky was quiet as he emptied the basin.

'Was it very long ago?' asked Martha.

'Six weeks,' said Micky, and Martha was shocked. She had assumed, somehow, that Micky's mother had been dead for years.

'If she was chased,' continued Micky, 'what I couldn't understand was why there were no other footprints.' He found a towel and dried his large hands. 'I didn't think of it till now.' He tucked the towel into a rubber stud on the edge of the worktop. 'What if whoever was behind her,' he whispered, 'didn't leave footprints, but just scuffs on the ground that I wouldn't have noticed?'

57

Martha felt her eyes widen, and she thought, with her flesh prickling, of the thing that walked like a man.

Micky was nodding his ginger head. 'Yes,' he said. 'Yes.'

Part II

Chapter 1

Blue sky hung among the trees. Snow slipped from branches and thudded into silence. Martha smiled at the beauty of it, though her face was arranged for weeping. A mile away, Daddy was buried; half-an-hour ago, as the church bells clanged eleven times, sending eleven chimes across the countryside.

She had wept, shivering in her new dress, inside her blue coat, snow creeping over her heels. They had walked home, mourners like a black crocodile wending through the trees, then curling hungrily around the dining tables.

Martha had escaped, changing her shoes for wellingtons, the utility room still smelling of bleach; sausage rolls the size of her big toe, hot in her hand, warm in her mouth, comfort in her stomach. And she smiled at the sunshine, and the blue shadows painted by the trees on the lumpy white ground.

'Martha!'

She turned. Micky, his jacket sleeve cut by a black band of mourning, came striding through the wood.

'Hi.' He grinned, and she took his hand. They wandered, eyes down against the sun's bright fingers, stepping over tree roots, seeing bony footprints sprinkled by birds, and standing still, when Micky tugged her hand, and his nod sent her glance searching the trees, and she found among high branches, three squirrels rushing in a row, tails fat as dandelions as they leapt from limb to limb. Martha smiled, hunching her shoulders, for she was delighted always with nature's beauty and abundant joy.

Micky stopped. 'It was here I found Mum's basket,' he whispered. They stared, then trudged on cutting a wandering trail in the white ground.

Martha wondered if she was old enough to fall in love. She held Micky's hand tightly, reminding herself that she didn't like ginger hair.

They stepped onto the perfect bulge of the high meadow where the standing stones waited for them. The sky was like blue paper with the meadow printed in white; and the great stones cast a giant shadow. 'It is forbidding!' cried Martha, and her voice, shrill and delicate, shattered against the stones and fell muffled into the snow-clad ground.

'I'm wearing my good shoes,' said Micky. 'Dad'll put a stranglehold on me, if I ruin 'em.' His mouth was pulled into a shape of ghastly terror and she leaned on his hand and smiled.

'We'll follow the trees,' she said, 'to the top of the hill. The snow's not so deep here. Then it's just a little distance to the stones. I don't want to go by myself.'

They moved on, ducking under branches. Martha stopped to press a snowball between her cupped palms. She threw it at Micky two steps away, and missed. The ball burst on the white blanket of the high meadow, spoiling its perfection.

Micky lobbed a soft lump of snow past her cheek and she screamed sending her delight splintering among the trees, and she fled carefully, until she fell on her hands, making sparkling cuffs on her blue coat.

At the top, the countryside dropped forever, a landscape of icing sugar, cracked by hedgerows and broken by tiny pop-up towns. Behind them was Martha's house at the bottom of the high meadow, its tall chimneys drawing smoky lines on the blue paper sky. Before them crouched Ruggens Dolmen, like a great beetle, waiting for meat.

Martha broke the snow by walking into it, crushing it under her wellingtons.

Their shadows slithered beside them, and the sun watched, rolling coldly across the sky the better to see them. The stone beetle paused.

Martha put her palm against the beetle's leg.

'Ruggens Dolmen,' said Micky.

Martha trudged round the stones and peered inside. The dolmen was three enormous stones placed upright in a triangle, with a fourth capstone on top.

'These are called sarsens,' she said.

'The stones?'

Martha nodded, and walked round out of his view. She talked under the beetle's tummy. 'It's from "Saracens", because Saracens were terribly foreign, and these stones are foreign to this countryside. They were brought here.'

'Pretty heavy,' said Micky.

'Tons and tons.' Martha's voice echoed slightly, and her cheeks chilled as she pressed her face into the gap between the stones. 'They may have been carried by glaciers and then made into a dolmen. It's a burial chamber,' she whispered wickedly.

'And I'm the ghost of the witch doctor!' boomed Micky, and Martha saw his mouth move in the shadowiness.

Her fingertips were in a groove. She lifted her face away from the gap, and sent her fingers exploring. She found a circle. Then another.

'What is it?' asked Micky. He reached up, scooped snow from the capstone, and hurled a snowball casually down the high meadow. Martha watched it flying dark against the bright sky. She thought it would never land, then it vanished silently into the white ground.

Beyond, at her house, someone ran.

A man, small as a bug in the distance, hurried a little way along the drive beside the stone-pillared wall of the lawn. Someone else dashed down the steps and stopped. More people came out.

'I say,' said Micky, 'your guests are leaving.'

Martha could see Mummy. She thought the first man was Jeff. The mourners left quickly, shaking hands with Mummy, then disappearing under the trees to use the pack horse trail, or walking rapidly down the drive. Someone else dashed from the house, called faintly to Jeff, turned to Mummy, then ran inside.

'Something's going on!' said Micky.

They began to run, but the snow held Martha's ankles. Only then did she realise how immensely strong Micky was; Daddy had carried her once from the kitchen all through the hall and up the stairs, panting, to her bedroom. Micky offered his arms and she stepped into them, and he lifted her in a sitting position and ran. Sure-footed he raced down the high meadow, thud-thudding on the white ground, snow flying from his feet, his breath feathering in the cold air. The sky danced wildly. Micky's arms were secure around her. Then his feet crackled through shrubbery and the corner of the hothouse skimmed Martha's beret. He dumped her feet-first on the steps as an ambulance ploughed along the drive.

Chapter 2

'Mummy, what is it?'

'Oh, Martha! Stand back, darling!'

The ambulance doors slammed then ambulance men opened the vehicle's rear doors and took a stretcher into the house. In a minute, they came carefully down the snowy steps, the stretcher rigid between them, a red blanket lumped over a body.

'Dr Bellamy!' said Martha, but the stretcher slid into the ambulance and the doors shut on her view of a bald head and grotesquely jutting beard. Dr Bellamy, Daddy's old friend, was unconscious.

A man, talking seriously to Mummy, swung on Martha, patted her shoulder with a hand that smelt like a doctor's hand, and hurried away. The ambulance wheels turned slowly printing their patterns in the snow, then only Jeff and Mummy were left, and Micky, and rooks cawing over the woods.

They went into the house. The rug at the hall fireplace was rumpled, and seemed to Martha to cower before the invasion of so many feet. Mummy pulled it flat. In the hearth lay a plastic bag. On the log pile was a stone, part of a larger square block, from the shape of it. Martha remembered the three bags beside the tumbled row of books on the mantelpiece. A whisky glass was on the mantelpiece and only two bags; this was the third in the hearth with the stone free of its plastic. On the stone someone had cut circles. Mummy reached towards it with both hands.

Bits of information rushed from Martha's memory into her mind. She felt again the circles under the yellow lichen on the sarsen stone. She remembered standing with Mummy at the bedroom window watching a dog-like shadow racing up the high meadow under the moonlight, fleeing towards Ruggens Dolmen. Mr McCorkindale had been shocked by a stone dug from his garden; and she remembered the stone stained red in the shaman's circle.

She just screamed.

She didn't scream in panic.

It was simply the quickest way to stop Mummy.

Mummy turned instantly, and her hazel eyes, worn with weeping at Daddy's funeral, were startled at seeing Martha calm, then annoyance weighted her fine dark eyebrows.

'Don't touch it!' said Martha. 'Don't you see what it is?'

'What what is?' asked Micky. Jeff's lips tightened under his moustache and his blue gaze demanded to know the meaning of this; his hand closed protectively on Mummy's arm.

More bits of information jumped at Martha. The whisky glass on the mantelpiece. The crumpled rug. The stone on the logs and the bag on the hearth; the ambulance men in and out in a minute. They couldn't have gone far into the house; just to the hall. As if she had seen it, she imagined little Dr Bellamy standing at the fire, putting his glass on the mantelpiece and lifting down the plastic bag. She saw him swing the bag, heavy with the stone onto the log pile, and topple the stone out. Then he touched it, and shock contracted his muscles, bruising his arm—like Mr McCorkindale—flinging him back, the plastic bag flying from his fingers, the rug skidding from his feet; sprawling horridly, bald head on oak floorboards, beard quivering upwards with electric energy.

'Don't you see?' Martha's whisper hung in the daylight

66

that stepped in to listen through the narrow windows; her words fell into dark corners; clattered among the wooden bones of chairs; danced with the hollow tick-tock of the grandfather clock. 'Don't you see?' she breathed, and they all turned, gazing fearfully on the stone with its one broken surface. 'We saw it in the circle. We saw the wolf walk round it. We saw it red and dreadful when the wolf was gone. Mummy, it's the shaman's stone. It's the stone of the werewolf!'

Chapter 3

Mummy put her hands behind her back. 'Are you sure?' she whispered. 'I almost touched it.'

Martha dragged off her beret and shook her hair. She sat low on a chair, prodding her coat buttons from their buttonholes, heeling off her wellingtons. She explained the rushing together of her thoughts.

'I say!' gasped Micky. 'She's a mini Sherlock Holmes! Better than I ever was! Is she right about the old man collapsing at the fire? I say! Well.' He frowned. 'Who put it in the bag?' He reached carefully towards the two bags beside the tumbled books and peered into their plastic mouths, carefully, like a dentist with small insane patients. 'They look like other bits of it,' he said.

'I suppose,' gasped Mummy as if she'd been holding her breath, 'Grant brought them.' Her dark curls moved with her head as she glanced at Martha.

'He must have,' said Martha.

'But how did he touch them without keeling over?' demanded Micky.

'This is too much!' moaned Mummy, and she sat in a chair and spread her hand over her eyes.

'Leave it for now,' said Jeff quietly. 'I'd better go. Angus'll be needing out.'

Thoughts and feelings flew around Martha's brain like splinters chopped from wood. She could weep. Or hug Mummy. Or punch Micky for going on about Daddy. And she was very hungry.

And angry.

She didn't know where the anger came from. It boiled into words and the words flew hot from her lips.

'Why is Daddy dead?'

'Martha!'

'He never hurt anyone!'

'I say—'

'And what does that thing want, creeping about our house? We should have stayed in London and this wouldn't have happened! It's all your fault!' she screamed at her mother. 'And Daddy's! It serves him right! It serves him right!'

And she fled, shocked at the hurt in Mummy's eyes, startled at Micky's look of fury, frightened at the words that flew in rage from her own mouth. She burst into her bedroom and fell face down on the bed, beating the pillow with her fists. Tears of anger and shame, tears of weariness tickled her nose. The pillow was cold. The quilt was cold through her new dress. Her arms and back lay warm in her good blue coat, and her hair trailed finely among her eyelashes.

She really didn't want her dress crushed. She rolled over and stood on the floor. A padded coathanger dangled from the mantelpiece. She slid the coat off, pretending that no tears were trailing warm lines down her face, and fitted the coathanger into her coat's shoulders. 'I will now hang you in the wardrobe!' she announced, then she hung her dress beside the coat and thought how well they looked.

She shouldn't have said such things. She stepped into her skirt, shook her head through a jumper, brushed her hair without looking in a mirror, and ran downstairs rubbing her face.

Mummy was in the kitchen but didn't turn round.

Martha hugged her so tightly that she cried out.

'It's all right,' said Mummy. 'I feel just as you do. But nobody's to blame—'

'I know!' whispered Martha. 'Where's Micky?' she asked.

'Tidying the drawing room. I'll bring some tea through. No point in sitting in the kitchen when the drawing room's warm. Check the fire, Martha, and, oh, someone spilled wine on the carpet—near the door. Take a bowl with hot water and washing up liquid—'

'Yes.'

'Rub it really hard, and there's an old towel in the utility room drawer. Once it's clean spread the towel on it and stand—'

'Yes!' Martha ran, the stone floor in the utility room curling her toes; then balancing frothy water through the kitchen, across the hall, knees bumping to the drawing room carpet; rub-rubbing on a pale stain, pushing up a line of fluff; Micky gathering plates and glasses. He turned his back on her, filling the room with silence, knocking a saucer on logs in the fire, and Martha guessed he was burning cigarette ends. Surely he could understand her outburst! Did she have to say sorry?

Empty wine bottles stood in a crowd. 'Jeff could have the bottles for his wine,' squeaked Martha. It wasn't an apology exactly, but it was all she could think of.

Micky faced her solemnly, and she waited on her knees, wet cloth cooling under her hand. Would he know she meant *sorry*?

'There's no need to grovel,' he said, 'but I think a cuddle is in order.' And she went to him, dripping bubbles from her fingers, and hugged him.

'Martha!'

'Oh!'

'You've left the cloth on the carpet.'

'She was saying sorry,' explained Micky.

'Oh, that's all right. Come and drink your tea.'

So Martha danced the towel into the wet carpet and sat at the table between her mother and Micky.

The snow fell in fat soft flakes, beautiful for walking through when you were snug inside an anorak, and with thick socks under wellingtons and a woolly hat that kept your ears warm but didn't make you deaf. They strolled beside the pillared wall that kept the gravel from the lawn. Then onto the road and were enclosed at once by hedgerows. Martha could no longer see the trees standing tall and grey above the pack horse trail, but she heard a rook complaining at the thinly falling sky. She saw the tyre tracks of the ambulance, and wondered how Dr Bellamy was. Behind her, in the house, by the hall fire, the stone still sat on the log pile.

Martha had loved London. But she loved the countryside more. She was awed by its silent distances, and the feeling of things waiting to grow. Leaves in the hedges excited her wonder and she decided to buy a book in Jeff's shop that would tell her the names of plants.

The hedges stopped, and cottages peered into the road from under snowy bonnets. And newer houses stood at the end of long drives. Then the road spread to include pavements and shops, though to Martha's London eyes there were few people and fewer cars.

A bus scraped from a lane, blinked away snowflakes, then growled and grumbled through the square. The church tower clanged quarter past one. In the churchyard, old gravestones, their lettering clogged white, ignored the noise but seemed to Martha to sink a little, and tilt with weariness. Daddy, she knew, was not there, but in the new cemetery beyond the bowling green.

The bus had stopped then groaned away leaving one passenger on the kerb, eyebrows wrinkled against the weather, gathering his coat collar. He saw Mummy.

'Mrs Lawson!'

'It's the vicar,' said Micky.

He hurried close, a little bundle of a man, his fat face changing expression every few seconds as if practising for different emotional events. His look of welcome dropped into concern. He shook Mummy's hand, then Micky's, then Martha's. 'We were lucky with the weather this morning,' he told them. 'Everything went smoothly. The service was satisfactory I trust? Splendid. The twenty-third psalm is quite my favourite. I must apologise again for not attending your buffet lunch, but there's trouble, as I told you, in the church.' His face folded into a mixture of worry and puzzlement. 'Not vandalism, exactly, but things knocked over, almost accidentally, and scratches on the wall near the vestry door—long, deep scratches—' He stared at the pavement as if the answer lay under the snow. '—perfectly visible, and—one hesitates to say it—but, quite disturbing. You see,' he declared, 'there's no way into the church!' And with a look of triumph, as if he'd baffled everyone with his cleverness, he tipped his hat and bundled away.

Martha smiled and Mummy's red lips opened, but before she could speak, the vicar who had dashed down the lane came hurrying back. Ten paces away, he stopped.

Martha, holding Mummy's hand and clutching Micky's elbow, waited. Snow flickered down blurring the ten paces between them.

72

The vicar's fat face held a genuine expression of horror.
'I think it's some animal!' he gasped.

Chapter 4

Snow silenced the world. A car slid past whispering at the white ground. A shop bell *ping*'d and died. Above them the dull gold of the church clock faded behind dropping flakes; and Martha felt that bodies in the graveyard were turning their shoulders up against the cold.

The vicar's cheeks fattened then drooped as his mouth went through its routine of expressions.

'Let us see it!' cried Mummy firmly.

The vicar's hand dropped from his collar to his pocket, and his collar fell open. 'You mean the church? Well . . . .' His hand crept out from the pocket, and he glanced down as if it weren't his. A large key lay across the palm. 'Of course!' He wheeled suddenly, and they hurried after him, the churchyard wall passing their knees, snow building on Martha's scarf, filling creases in the arms of her anorak. Their feet destroyed the perfection of the path that curved to the church door. A yew tree leaned towards them, nudging Micky's shoulder, sparking snow at his head.

Hidden by the vicar's black body, the lock thumped. Then one half of the door swung in, dark as a beetle's wing. The vicar stood aside and Mummy led through the porch with its stack of hymn books and a forgotten bowler hat, past the inner door and onto paths of rush matting that would guide the congregation quietly among the pews.

They waited, facing this way and that, as the vicar fumbled to open the other beetle's wing, then he hooked back the inner door letting cold air fall into the church, making Mummy shiver and Micky move his feet restlessly. Angles of light pointed down from windows, slanted across the brooding pew backs, bumped against pillars dropping shadows behind them. The vicar's hand found a mass of brass switches and slid down with a ripple of clicks, and needle-sharp points of light bit the gloom.

'This way!' he urged, but rather than lead, he herded them, like a fat nervous sheep dog with three uncertain sheep, and they wandered, Mummy, Martha and Micky, sideways, glancing back, to see where his plump white hands were gesturing.

It was only a little way to the far corner of the church, Micky ducking beneath the beak of the lectern eagle, Martha fingering the ribs of a column that swept up arching under the church tower, Mummy patting the carved font with her mittened palm.

'Over there,' said the vicar, and his voice was a hush of awe and terror, and Martha watched his twisting mouth, his shifting brows, and was astonished to see sweat glittering from under his hair. Beyond, through the open door, a yew tree stood dark in the descending snow.

'Right in the corner! Low down!'

Martha turned and at once saw scratches deep in the stonework, and she knelt, reaching out. Then she remembered Mummy stretching for the stone on the hearth, and hesitated.

Silence hung in the church.

Micky was crouched beside Martha, his tough face relaxed. Mummy stood very still, shoulders hunched against the cold, reminding Martha of herself. The vicar had edged backwards to the doorway, a black fidgeting bundle haloed in daylight, with the yew tree peering over his shoulder.

Martha turned to stare at the scratches. She knew what had caused them. She had known even before the vicar had

75

mentioned an animal.

Below the scratches was a curve on an untouched stone; a short deliberate curve like a sour mouth, dim light on its lower lip. Martha leaned close, and saw that the curve completed itself downwards into a circle. She saw another circle. And portions of a third and fourth.

She was looking at another piece of the shaman's stone. The scratches were all around it, as if something had tried to dig the stone free.

She shuddered and stood up quickly.

'Perhaps we should go!' cried the vicar and he glanced up. High over his head bright bulbs, held in a circle of iron, swung on a chain, clinking and creaking. 'The wind's getting up.' Martha couldn't see his face against the daylight but his fat outline changed shape as he cringed. Behind him, curiously, the snow fell with no flurries of wind.

A second light began to swing. In the porch a hymn book flicked open, and its pages rattled like birds' wings. The vicar cried out and pressed against the fluted stone of the inner doorway.

The second light creaked, and others began to sway.

Micky's jaw was grim, but he faced around boldly, while Mummy stood pale, her little hands tight before her. Martha refused to be frightened. In her mind she defied the swinging creaking lights. Her mouth was rigid, her cheeks aching with tension, but she stood, not even holding Mummy's arm.

Light slipped in over window-sills filling the church with crouching darkness.

Bong!

In the tower, high in the snowy day, the clock clanged half past one. The vicar's mouth pulled wide and he dashed from

76

the cold comfort of the doorframe, past the fluttering hymn book, into the dropping white air. Martha's breath hissed between her teeth. Mummy's hands twisted in their mittens and her hazel eyes searched the shadows. Micky appeared not to notice the chime, but kept turning, expecting danger.

The lights swung wildly scarring bright lines in the gloom.

'We must leave!' whispered Mummy.

Martha's lips squeezed together. She didn't move. One of the beetle-wing doors crashed shut, blocking daylight, brightening the rushing points of light. The pile of hymn books heaved uneasily.

'If the other door shuts . . .' said Mummy, and she sidled away.

Martha followed, reluctant to give up, but relieved, for she was really very afraid.

'There!' urged Micky, and his arm went across Martha as he grabbed Mummy's shoulder. He pointed.

A hassock came sliding from under the pews, tripped on the matting and tumbled to Martha's feet like a playful dog; but Micky was pointing higher, down the nave, towards the rood screen. On the pulpit steps, light and sloping shadow thickened, and a head turned balefully, its jaws issuing a thin and distant howl like a soul in anguish. Glaring down on them was the monstrous form of the thing that walked like a man, stronger even than Jefferson Wilson, more ancient than the walls of the little church, and more savage than any living animal—the werewolf.

Chapter 5

They fled. The bowler hat rolled out at their heels and cowered beside a glass dome full of dead flowers.

Micky pulled the door shut, and came backwards along the path. On the pavement the vicar was frantic in a knot of villagers who listened, shoulders white, looking vaguely towards the church.

The vicar's arms thrust at Mummy. His mouth opened to speak then it pulled out of shape and he glared fiercely. 'I ran for help!' he declared, and snow melted on Martha's tongue as she gaped. She had never heard such a lie!

'Perhaps you'd better lock up,' suggested Mummy. 'Thank you for letting us see round.' And she marched past taking Martha firmly by the wrist.

As they crossed the square, the church bell clanged dismally. Martha looked back. Through the snowflakes she glimpsed the clock. 'It's just chimed one thirty-four,' she said, and Micky grinned.

They stood close to a brilliant shop window gazing back through the snow and sliding traffic. The knot of villagers was unravelling and in a minute the vicar had an audience of just one large woman. A van put its square green body in their way, and when it was past, the large woman was marching towards the church door while the vicar flapped nervously on the pavement.

'I say!' gasped Micky. 'She'd better not go in there!' But the traffic was a barricade trapping him in the gutter. The woman vanished into the church, and the vicar's voice came in pieces between vehicles. Then the beetle-wing doors ejected the woman. She turned, pulled them shut, advanced past the yew tree shaking her head, spoke to the vicar, who stopped dancing, and walked off. The vicar hesitated forlornly as if seeking help. He saw Mummy and walked up the path, his black body stiff.

'He's locking up,' said Micky.

'He didn't go in!' said Martha and turned her back.

In the shop window was her name, MARTHA LAWSON, in red letters on a pale blue sheet of card. The other letters were in black:

CHARLOTTE UNDER THE HILL
by
LOCAL AUTHORESS
MARTHA LAWSON

'Mummy!'

On Mummy's cheek, just below her eye, a melted snowflake glistened. She squeezed Martha's shoulder. Six copies of the book shone out at them very smart in their dark blue jackets.

'We set it up this morning,' said Micky, 'before we came to the service. I designed the card last night while *someone* was snoring her little head off.'

'It's very good,' said Mummy.

'Thank you!' whispered Martha and her shoulders came up as excitement thrilled through her chest. 'Can we go in?'

Micky opened the shop door, which *ping*'d a bell. 'We don't close during lunch because that's the only time some customers can come.'

Jeff was smiling over the till, wrapping a book. He saw them. 'Be with you in a minute. Six pounds ninety-five, please.'

Angus welcomed them with his tail and tongue, then returned to his place beside Jeff. Martha browsed, immediately lost, moving tilt-headed along rows of books, approving of the keen straight shelves, new beneath the bulging plaster of the black-beamed ceiling. She smiled. It was the sort of shop for lingering in all day. Especially, she thought, when the best position in the window displayed her book! Did these people, she wondered, glancing around the other browsers, realise an author was amongst them! Her smile widened then she forgot everything but her exploration of titles.

She found a big book on *Egypt—The Ancient Land*, and it reminded her of Daddy, for Egyptology was his hobby. She pushed her mittens into her anorak pocket and drew the book from between its neighbours. It was too large and heavy to hold easily, so she opened it onto an old-fashioned school teacher's desk that came as high as the knot in her scarf. She had to reach to turn the pages, and the paper slid cool and beautiful beneath her fingers. Minutes vanished into the wonderfully coloured illustrations.

She let the book shut. Something bumped in her memory, and she stroked open pages near the front. She didn't know what she'd seen, but something . . . .

And there it was.

In heavy type.

Anubis.

The word Daddy had written in his diary. And she stared at the picture of Anubis and realised that Daddy had not really dreamed of an Egyptian god draped in gold, sitting on a throne; for though Anubis had a dog's head and a man's body, Daddy, she knew, had dreamt of a monster even more ancient, but too untamed for clothing, and too terrible for worship.

Her breath shuddered.

Chapter 6

Tears took her by surprise. They splashed onto the page of Anubis, and Martha dragged her mittens from her pocket and dabbed the god dry. She hadn't wept since morning, at the graveside. It suddenly seemed wrong that she should be in a bookshop, that Mummy should be talking to Jeff. The universe ought to be holding its breath; time itself should freeze, its moments locked in mourning for Daddy.

Martha kept her head down and sobbed quietly, mittens on her cheeks, Anubis a coloured blur. She found a hankie and blew her nose. She held the mittens on her eyes to blot the last tears. She hoped no one had noticed.

But while she'd wept, the bit of her mind that watched had been thinking, and Martha saw that Daddy's illness came from the stone. The stone had caused his 'dream of Anubis'.

Her lips were a hard bar of flesh. She had decided. She would read Daddy's diary.

She began her search for a book on plants.

Martha's nose was comfortably cold as Mummy unlocked the door of their house. Micky tapped his toes on a step to knock off snow. Martha sat in the doorway and let him tug at her wellingtons, and as she sat back propped on rigid arms she remembered the scraping of the creature's claws on the stained glass, and how, in the dim light, she had seen nothing. Now, in the cold luminescence of this winter's day, three little lines attracted her eye. They were not on the glass but on the lead strips that held the red and green roses in place, and they were just the same space apart, thought

82

Martha, as the scores on the stones inside the church.

She smiled up at Micky. They closed the door on the falling snow. Mummy was kicking a log firmly onto embers in the fireplace. She stepped back hurriedly, shuddering. 'Ooh! That thing gives me the creeps,' she said, and the stone with its broken end and simple ring pattern was quite the wickedest thing Martha had ever seen.

Micky shrugged uncomfortably. 'I can put it outside.'

'You'll do no such thing!' said Mummy sternly. 'Not until we know more about it! But you might cover it up. I'll put the kettle on. Oh, no! There's still the drawing room to tidy and a million dishes to wash! And poor Dr Bellamy's glass is still on the mantelpiece.' And she glanced at Micky helplessly, letting him approach the stone and scoop the glass away.

'Ugh!' he said. 'It does reach out t'you! I didn't notice before. D'you think its power's growing?'

Growing.

The idea scratched Martha's back with icy fingernails. She let the zip of her anorak trickle open as she thought. She took out her book on plants.

'Perhaps,' she said, 'the plastic bag has been shielding us. Then Dr Bellamy drained the power by touching it.'

'Now it's back to normal!' gasped Micky.

'There's a rubber floor mat in the utility,' suggested Martha thinking of how to stop the stone's influence.

'We'll try it!' said Micky, and left a breeze as he dashed away.

The air in the library hung cold, making the ancient books huddle for warmth in their shelves. Daddy's books, snug in the grocery boxes, listened to the door closing and Martha's soft stockinged tread on the carpet.

The two fireplaces were wide and low and the fires set with paper, twigs and long thick logs. Armchairs, fat and slack with age, stared at the backs of the chimneys. Martha padded to the desk, put down her book, and lifted Daddy's lighter. She pressed the ignition and a tall flame startled her eyes. Then something changed, like a familiar sound that you only hear when it stops; but it wasn't a sound that had stopped.

Of course.

She shut off the flame, and walked back to the door. Micky had put the rubber mat over the stone. That was what had changed. The whispers of wickedness were smothered.

She closed the door. The library felt warmer. The darkness had gone, along with the stone's influence. She ran to a fireplace and sent the lighter's flame bursting hungrily into the paper. Twigs flared, tips turning to ash like thin cigars, but roaring fiercely.

She sauntered towards the desk, leaving fingermarks on the drum table, shaking a curtain then hurrying from under a fall of dust. She sat in Daddy's chair. Her chair. She pulled the drawer and lifted the diary onto her lap. She slid the drawer closed, and opened another. She took out paper. Daddy's gold pen and silver pencil shone gently on the desk. Martha chose the pen, gathered up the paper and diary and began walking past bookshelves, going the long way towards the fire. She needed something to lean on. Something thin. There's a thin one. No title, but wonderfully strong in leather, green and red. She hooked a finger onto it and pulled. But it was stuck. She sighed, and suddenly her emotions simmered like water in a pan, threatening to boil, so she left the books and curled into a slack armchair, pretending the chair was warm on her skin; the logs sent flares of heat against her knees and face. She opened the diary.

Chapter 7

She didn't move. The fire banged and popped like a distant gunfight. Daddy's writing was very difficult. Martha leaned her paper on the chair's broad arm and copied some of Daddy's sentences. She left out dates and technical remarks. She wanted to know what Daddy felt.

The chair warmed her. Her knees began to scorch. At last, she straightened her legs, rose, switched on the lights and crossed to Daddy's desk.

The seat was low, so she borrowed cushions from the armchairs; now her elbows were level with the typewriter. She lifted the typewriter (which was very heavy) and everything else, onto the carpet.

She left the room and returned; she sprayed white puddles of polish onto the desk and rubbed very fast with a duster. She left the duster and polish at the door so she wouldn't forget them. She replaced the typewriter, Daddy's photograph of Stonehenge, the silver pencil and the gold pen. The lighter and ashtray went onto the mantelpiece above the mumbling fire; the microscope became an ornament on a window-sill.

Martha sat down and removed the cover from the typewriter. It was her desk now.

Extract from Daddy's Diary

I certainly wasn't keen on starting a dig at this time of year, especially on such an open site, but Torkie [That's Daddy's friend, Dr Bellamy.] insists we can cope. He had miles of plastic for protecting excavations, and a sackful of tent pegs. He won't say where they came from—the old rascal.

Everything is going well, I suppose. Some new post holes uncovered.

Too cold today in my opinion, but Torkie just burrows away. With his sleeves up! Everyone laughed at Palmiston when he tripped, tried to grab His Majesty [I think Daddy means the King Stone.] slipped and ripped his jeans from knee to ankle. He swore considerably and challenged everyone to show him exactly what had torn his jeans. No one paid any attention, but he was suitably mollified when little Bessie sewed him up. Now he can't keep his eyes off her.

Part of the trouble, besides the cold, is the short day. We simply can't afford lights, so outdoor work ceases around 3.30 pm. And the road worries me. No street lights, of course, out here, and only a scattering of traffic, but some of us are getting too familiar with the road—in other words, careless. Had to tear a strip off young Benson-Forbes for sitting in the middle of the tarmac eating his lunch! If only all the stones were on one side of the road—but the King Stone is to the north, nearer the barrows. I don't like the look of it.

We are finding very little. The King Stone is terrible in the fading light. Palmiston, working near it, stood up and stretched; for a moment I saw him as an animal; reminded me of something from an old horror movie. The Rollright Stones have never had a good reputation. I think they're affecting me, though I am the least superstitious man I know—except perhaps for Torkie. I don't believe he is afraid of anything.

I don't know why I wrote that. There is nothing to fear. We are very lucky; there has been no rain, though the sky has threatened all day.

Of all the bad luck! Palmiston is ill! Says he felt it coming on over the past few days. He looks all right but his eyes slide about a bit as if he was expecting someone to creep up on him.

It's lonely working beside the King Stone. Sunshine today but the shadow of the stone is like a cold blanket on my back. Bessie has turned her maternal instincts towards me—she brought my tea for the second time.

I knew that road would bring trouble! I insisted to Torkie that rope barriers should be put up to make people go round them. Bessie had brought my tea and stepped out almost into a car. She claims something moved just behind her, making her jump. There was certainly nothing there for I was sitting watching her over my mug. I wish she wouldn't put in so much sugar.

Some silly ass said the site is haunted. Now the younger ones are practically walking about backwards in their attempts to see behind them. Bessie swore that someone was hiding at the back of the farmer's toll hut. Torkie good-naturedly had a look but found nothing except more chickens.

This morning my plastic sheeting was torn. May have been a cat from the house at the corner.

I think the cold's getting to me—however, I uncovered something, and that revived my energy. The surface of a stone. It's about two feet down and definitely an artefact. I haven't touched it. The soil fell away from it and I brushed the corner clear. I'm not sure why I haven't touched it. The sky is very overcast and uneasy. So is everyone here—except Torkie. I think he has no nerves.

That fool Benson-Forbes is wearing a crucifix. I told him to hide his stupidity under his shirt. The others are nervous

88

enough without *that* on display!

No matter where I position myself, the shadow of the King Stone always manages to arrange itself across my back. My find is clear of the surrounding earth. It is certainly man-made with a cup and ring pattern. It measures 26cm by 10cm and is approximately 15cm from the flat end to the broken end.

Today, uncovered two smaller pieces of the stone. There is obviously another large piece somewhere, perhaps bigger than this piece. It certainly isn't nearby. We may never find it. The cold is surely affecting me.

Still haven't touched any of the three pieces. I don't like to mention this to Torkie—he's so unassailably practical, but the fact is—I'm scared. I'm beginning to look over my shoulder now.

Bessie has stopped bringing my tea. She apologised, very much embarrassed, but quite adamant. She swears there's something alive near the King Stone—something that manages to keep just out of sight. How that can be I'm blessed if I know. There's not a thing on this side of the road to hide behind except the stone. I can see at least three counties from here.

Very tired. Strange dream last night, but couldn't recall it. Will not move the stones until I get something to put them in, and I will wear gloves. Must warn Martha and Jill not to touch them, but I must get them home for study! I feel drained. I suppose moving house is taking it out of me.

Left the site early and went to a hotel in Chipping Norton for a whisky. Not my style, but I needed it. One must face reality. Perhaps old age is creeping up on me! Though I was only 37 last birthday. Or perhaps 38.

I have remembered the plastic bags at last. The weather

will break soon, then we'll be in for a storm.

Martha and Jill are the most precious things in my life. I don't know why I'm writing this. It's not as if I'm actually dying of old age! But I am exhausted.

Stones are home. Inadvertently touched the smallest piece. I was right to avoid contact. Nasty sensation. Left the blasted things on the hall mantelpiece. Haven't the strength to put them anywhere more secure. Bed calls. Why do I have the feeling this is my last cigar?

Definitely ill. Not imagination—though if I breathe deeply I can appear all right, so Jill and Martha have noticed nothing. Terribly drained. Maybe just 'flu. If I don't feel better tomorrow, will consult a doctor. I wonder what he can do for dreams of Anubis. I think I am terrified.

Chapter 8

The door clicked and Micky appeared at the desk with a glass of milk and sandwiches left from the buffet. 'I've been told not to disturb you,' he whispered and paced away. As he reached the door Martha asked what date his mum had died, and his voice held a question as he answered; but she didn't explain, and she didn't hear him go.

The date Micky's mum had been chased through the wood was the date the dig began at the Rollright Stones.

Everything began then.

As if the first probing trowel splitting the grass had sent a shock through the earth, stirring the power of the shaman's stone, awakening the millennial sleep of the werewolf. Which came from Ruggens Dolmen.

Martha went through the desk drawers. Daddy had maps of all the places he worked. She found the one centred on Chipping Norton. She spread it on the carpet at the fire and ate her sandwiches and sipped her milk while she studied. The Rollright Stones. Each stone was marked, the actual stone circle standing south of the road that was the boundary between Oxfordshire and Warwickshire. North of the road was the great monolith, the King Stone. She slid her finger and found Ruggens Dolmen.

Her own house was marked and Jeff's cottage, and the pack horse trail. She wondered how old the pack horse trail really was. Could it go back to Neolithic times? For if it did, perhaps it had led from Ruggens Dolmen to the Rollright Stones, for though it was only three hundred metres long today it pointed straight from the dolmen to the stone circle. Perhaps it meant nothing, but Martha shivered, then found she'd eaten the last sandwich.

The shaman's stone was the key to everything. Martha knew where each piece was. The three bits Daddy had dug up were just through the door in the hall. A piece was under the snow in Mr McCorkindale's garden, and the other big piece was in the church; whoever had built the church had found the stone handy and cemented it into the wall.

She crackled the map flat and her searching finger pointed at the tiny cross that was the church. It was in line with the pack horse trail. Ruggens Dolmen, Mr McCorkindale's garden, the church, and the King Stone at Rollright. A straight line! Probably the church was built on ancient sacred ground, a special place, known since prehistory.

There was now only one problem. Martha leaned back on the carpet and let her eyes wander around the wood panelling on the ceiling. Should the pieces of stone be brought together? Or should Jeff and Micky pound them to dust, their mighty muscles sparkling with sweat while the snow melted on their hot skin . . . .

Martha blinked. She did think the silliest things!

'Dr Bellamy's coming,' said Mummy. 'Didn't you bring your glass and plate?'

'But he's in hospital!'

'That's what *I* said, but he's discharged himself. He asked what the roads were like and I said I thought the Range Rover could get through—'

'Is it still snowing?' Martha saw snowflakes swinging onto the black kitchen window. She hadn't noticed night come creeping around the house.

'—and,' sighed Mummy, 'I directed him to Horseshoe Cottage because that's where we'll be—' She put her arms out and Martha snuggled close. Neither wanted to speak. The plastic in the window frame flapped slightly, and Micky came in balancing Martha's dishes and clutching the polish and duster.

'Fires are secure,' he announced.

'Dr Bellamy's coming,' said Martha.

'I know,' said Micky. 'The butler answered the phone.' And the butler inclined his ginger head respectfully as he conveyed the dishes to the sink.

They left the hall light on, and Martha paused at the fence posts, topped now with ridiculous hats of snow. She looked back, reluctant to leave her home, and saw the square glow of the front door filled with rushing feathers. She walked on encouraged by Micky's hand round hers. Horseshoe Cottage would be safer.

The snow was too thick, like a carpet of cotton wool, for Martha to feel the cobbles of the trail. She imagined the startling clatter of hooves a hundred years ago, scattering birds from the undergrowth as packmen rode by, saddles creaking under mysterious burdens. Or had small men walked here, padding the earth flat with generations of their naked feet, men who would die thousands of years before Jesus, thousands of years, even, before Anubis? Perhaps here, between Ruggens Dolmen and the Rollright Stones, Anubis was born, in a strange ceremony with a shaman, a wolf and a stone; circles within circles.

Lights glimmered ahead.

'We'll use the kitchen door,' said Micky. 'It'll be unlocked.' They trudged wellington-deep down the side of the cottage, under brows of thatch fat with snow, slightly startled by the ghost of a holly tree.

93

Far away, Martha heard a car engine moaning. A pot clattered in the kitchen, and when Micky pushed the door inwards, warmth and the taste of hot food spilled into the night.

'I say!' declared Micky. 'Fish and chips—'

'Sssh!' said Martha.

'I could eat a whale—'

'Listen!' insisted Martha and they listened, Jeff coming to the door, a fish slice in his large hand, and a woman's apron decorating his chest and stomach.

'I hear a car,' said Mummy.

'There's someone sobbing!' said Micky, and the sobbing rose to a howl, and light split the window in the next cottage; the door rattled open and Mrs McCorkindale shrieked across the soft white space. 'It's my Donald!' she cried. 'Donald! I think he's dying! Help me! I think he's dying!'

Chapter 9

Jeff ran into the snow. Micky and Mummy hesitated. The car growled close, beams from its headlights glancing among the trees. It was a Range Rover, and it spun as it braked, deluging the snow with brilliance, dropping hard shadows from the fence, shrubs and people. The engine stopped, the brilliance vanished, leaving the dim street lamp and yellow splashes from inside the cottages. Then Dr Bellamy strode among them, for a moment, small as a gnome in a bloated anorak, but really, taller than Mummy.

Then Mummy told him what had just happened and he ordered everyone politely indoors, then followed Jeff to the McCorkindales' cottage. Martha found she was holding the fish slice.

Mummy took charge of the kitchen, heaving her coat into Martha's arms, rescuing the fish from a smoke-filled pan, flapping about the tiled floor in her wellingtons, making sure her butler was setting the table properly.

'I thought he was an archaeologist?' said the butler. Martha hung their clothes in the cloakroom between the kitchen and loo, placing her wellingtons side-by-side with Micky's, to drain.

'So he is,' said Mummy. 'He qualified in medicine years ago, but didn't practise. He prefers dead people, he says, to sick ones. We'd better eat—this fish is drying up, and the chips are past their best. Is there a tin of peas anywhere?'

Angus said, 'Wuff!' as Jeff came in, snow on his eyebrows, his front still frilly with the apron.

'Oh, how is he?' cried Mummy. 'And how is Dr Bellamy? He should be in hospital!'

95

'I think Donald's all right. And there's nothing wrong with Bellamy! Takes charge like a born officer! I thought he was an archaeologist? Oh, I see. I say, we'd better eat that fish before it turns to shoe leather!'

Dr Bellamy, sitting very straight in Jeff's armchair, fumbled in his waistcoat pockets. He found a box of Swan Vestas and laid it carefully on his knee. His fingers dug awkwardly until he grunted and nudged out a tiny pipe; the bowl was as yellow as butter, the stem a curve of ivory. To Martha, he was a gnome. A kind, slightly distant little man, but with a gnome's twiggy fingers, and a gnome's dry face; and the face watched everything over its beard, and thought its thoughts inside its bald head; a man Daddy had liked very much.

'He certainly looked as if he was dying.' Dr Bellamy's glance touched everyone, then returned to the ritual of cleaning and filling the pipe. 'But he's not. I don't think I'm breaking any confidences by saying that people can die of boredom—or fear.' He knocked a dottle of tobacco onto the stove. 'Says he saw a wolf walking like a man—in his living room. Anyone know anything about that?' He stared at Angus.

Mummy reached for Martha's hand. Micky and Jeff glanced at each other.

'And of course he had touched the stone.' The doctor thumbed fresh tobacco into his pipe. 'I touched a stone. But I'm not an old man with nothing to do but be afraid. I know you have something to tell me, because none of you showed any surprise when I mentioned the wolf man.' His forehead wrinkled, a match exploded in his fingers and he rolled the flame over the tobacco.

Jeff began, his soft moustache fluffing as he spoke of the prowler in the moonlight; then Mummy told how the creature pushing through the garden had become a dog-like shadow racing towards Ruggens Dolmen. Jeff very quietly explained the breaking of the kitchen window, and Micky burst out with what had happened in the church.

The doctor's expression had been slightly superior in his kindly way, but as the story grew, his gnome's face crumpled around his pipe, and he fingered Martha's extract from Daddy's diary very thoughtfully indeed.

'I think,' he said at last, 'we'll have a look at the stones.' And he pushed the pipe to the corner of his mouth and stood up. 'There's no need for anyone to come. If you'll give me the house key, Jill, I'll fetch them.'

'But they attract that creature!' cried Mummy. 'We came here to be safe!'

'Mm,' said the doctor, and waited until Mummy handed him the key.

'Look here, Doctor—' puffed Jeff.

'Torkie,' suggested the doctor. 'Could you get my anorak, Martha?' Then he was a gnome swollen by the anorak, puffing smoke from his yellow pipe. He opened the kitchen door, facing the night. 'Do you think,' he said into the darkness, 'you could find the stone in your neighbour's garden? Back soon.' And he vanished round the edge of the doorway.

'I'll go!' cried Micky.

'I'll hold the torch!' said Martha. 'It'll be all right, Mummy! Daddy will look after us. And Jeff,' she said, and gave him a special hug.

In the little cloakroom, Martha stomped into her wellingtons, and Angus helped by snuffling her knees. She struggled

97

into her anorak and zipped it tight to the chin. She felt for her mittens and found the writing pad with her poem. Then Micky crushed in, pushing a torch into her fingers, and she tried again to read Daddy's words, squashed against Angus's fur and avoiding Micky's elbows.

'*Rollright*!' she gasped. 'It was in Daddy's diary! The same scribble!' Her mittened paw underlined the writing. '*Rollright* something *return*!'

'It can't be a proper sentence,' said Micky.

'Rollright must return,' suggested Martha.

'That doesn't make sense.'

'Is the middle word "hurry"?' said Martha.

'Worry?'

'Bury. It's bury!'

'What are you up to in there?' Mummy's voice, bright from the kitchen.

'Mummy, look!' They gathered in the kitchen around the white square of Martha's pad, peering, repeating the words. Rollright. Bury. Return.

'Well,' said Jeff, 'that's clear enough. The stones go back to Rollright. Bury them where they belong.'

'What about the one in the garden?' asked Micky. 'Should we put it where Mr McCorkindale found it, or take it to Rollright with the rest?'

And they talked; and as they talked, things clicked in Martha's brain; facts, ideas, events came together, and she knew why the shaman's stone was scattered between Rollright and Ruggens Dolmen, and she understood the presence of the werewolf.

'It's very simple,' she said to herself, and Jeff lowered his voice and was quiet.

'Out with it,' said Micky.

'The stone was broken up to destroy the werewolf's power—'

'Of course!' groaned Jeff.

'And now that thing's trying to gather up the pieces!' cried Micky.

'And Daddy disturbed it,' whispered Mummy.

'Each stone goes back where it came from,' growled Jeff. 'Now. Micky—'

'I'll do next door!'

'Remember not to touch it!' cried Mummy.

The snow had stopped. Martha held onto Micky as they staggered shin-deep up the garden. Martha looked back. Between the cottages the Range Rover stood cold beneath the lamp-post.

'He must have walked,' whispered Martha, and swung the torch forwards and her stomach thrilled with fear for another light, just ahead, glimmered in the darkness. But Micky strode on and she realised it was the torch face reflected in the greenhouse; in the greenhouse Micky found a spade, then they climbed a low wall, crunchy with ivy, soft with snow.

'He was digging about there,' said Micky. Martha heard a grin in his voice. 'There's Dr Bellamy!' he whispered, and she moved her mouth into a smile, for 'Dr Bellamy' was a spade stuck in the ground, wearing a man's hat on its handle.

'The stone must be near,' said Martha. Micky scooped away snow leaving the earth naked to the torch's beam.

One or two flakes tumbled past the sweeping spade.

'There!' said Martha crouching close.

Micky scraped soil from the stone. It had two flat sides, one carved with part of a circle.

The hat on Mr McCorkindale's spade moved.

'Wind's coming up,' said Micky and struck deep, digging fast. 'Here's the hole the stone was in. I hope the road to Rollright isn't blocked.' More flakes fell through the torch beam. 'Burying the bits of stone your dad dug up should finish this business.'

The hat turned on the spade, but Martha couldn't feel any breeze.

Micky heaved up soil. 'That's deeper than the old man will ever dig.' He clunked the stone with the spade, knocking it into the hole.

The hat lifted and spun into the darkness.

For a moment they stood, Martha's circle of light finding the hat. Snowflakes fell straight down. 'There's no wind,' she said.

Micky shovelled furiously, burying the stone, stamping the earth flat.

Mr McCorkindale's spade dropped sideways and twisted as if it were dying. Masses of snow slid from the cottage roofs, booming dully against the ground.

They heard a voice, and stared towards the streetlight.

'Help!' came faintly from the trees.

'It's Dr Bellamy!' gasped Martha.

Chapter 10

'Get Dad!' shouted Micky, and he was running and leaping through the garden, between the cottages, round the Range Rover . . . .

Martha screamed. She ran screaming. The kitchen door tore open. Jeff loomed massive in the light.

'It's coming!' she yelled. 'Help them!'

Jeff disappeared, then plunged past holding a shotgun. He raced towards the pack horse trail, Angus loping at his side.

Mummy tried to take Martha into the house. 'No!' Martha shook her off. 'We must get to Rollright! Mummy, we must go now!'

A shot cracked in the darkness and Mummy's hazel eyes widened. Immediately she took Martha past the cottage and onto the road. They opened the Range Rover's doors.

'Get in the back!' gasped Mummy.

Martha slid the window open and leaned out.

Mummy, in her dress and wellingtons, was hurrying towards the trail.

She stopped. Her hands flew to her cheeks. Another shot banged and Martha saw the flash. Mummy screamed at everyone to get into the Range Rover.

They came frantically from the trees, Jeff with the gun and a handful of swinging plastic; Micky, fantastically, carrying the little doctor, as he had carried Martha down the high meadow.

'The car keys!' screamed Martha. 'The car keys!'

Micky slammed the doctor into the front seat while Jeff rushed to the driver's door. Micky and Mummy tumbled into the back. Martha leaned forward. She pulled the keys from the doctor's pocket and stuffed them into Jeff's palm.

Something wicked came from the undergrowth. Low, it came, dark as shadows. 'The window!' screamed Martha. It leapt.

Micky jerked the glass shut, and the Range Rover roared defiantly and slid away, but the vehicle rocked as the awful thing struck the side. For a second Martha saw two red points of light, and from the rear window she watched a shape sprawling darkly beneath the lamp-post.

Then she realised.

'Where's Angus?!' she gasped. She grabbed Jeff's shoulder. 'Stop!' she screamed. 'We've left Angus!'

But Jeff drove on, and Micky turned his face to the glass. A horrid emptiness filled Martha's brain.

'He saved our lives,' whispered Micky. 'That thing's stronger than all of us.'

And Martha's eyes overflowed and she beat the seat with her fists.

The Range Rover growled over unrecognisable roads. White trees dashed into the headlights; hedgerows ran alongside. Mummy wept. Micky snapped the shotgun closed.

'Break it open again,' ordered Jeff quietly, and Micky obeyed.

The doctor's bald head jerked, and he sighed.

Mummy drew in a deep breath. She touched his shoulder. 'Are you all right?'

The doctor's fingers climbed up and patted Mummy's hand. 'I'll never be sure of anything again,' he said quietly. 'Yes. I'm all right. But that marvellous dog of yours. I must

102

thank him. He tore that brute off me . . . .'

Despite the engine's noise and the rattle of things in the dark, silence joined the five people like a thick rope; silence that told a story and asked for sympathy. 'I'm so sorry,' whispered the doctor.

Martha was glad when the Range Rover stopped. Jeff reversed into a layby. He parked at an angle to let the headlights blaze across the road. Beyond a thin hedge stood the King Stone.

'Anyone think to bring a spade?' asked Jeff.

'I always carry one in this weather. In the back . . . .' The doctor's face was pale.

Jeff faced Martha and Micky. 'We all die,' he said softly. 'We can't die better than Angus, giving his life for someone else.' Then he clattered violently into the night, and everyone followed in a huddle of knees and hands, and the shotgun and the shovel.

They left holes in the snow with their feet; they crushed through the hedge into Warwickshire, sending their shadows ahead as if to test the King's temper. But the great stone seemed to have turned its back and was contemplating the vast darkness of a landscape speckled by tiny distant lights.

'The King refused his crown of snow,' sighed Martha and laid her palm on his side. 'It's hot!' she cried.

Jeff leapt and pulled her away.

Martha gasped, 'No wonder there's no snow on top! Feel it!'

Their fingers tiptoed on the stone, Micky and the doctor walking round to the darkside, as daring as astronauts circling the moon.

'We must get on!' cried Mummy, and Jeff hauled back the polythene sheeting laid down by Martha's father to protect the site. The fragments of the shaman's stone, now gathered in one plastic carrier bag, dented the white ground.

'Is this the spot? Doctor!'

Something changed.

Mummy's fingers closed coldly on Martha's wrist. The snow stopped. The King's shadow reached far into the night. The moon slid from behind a cloud and gazed down, its gentle light bright in Martha's eyes. Jeff was crouched over the hole grasping the spade which looked like a fantastic weapon of polished silver. Micky and the doctor stood still, quiet and still.

'I think we should hurry!' gasped the doctor. He turned to Jeff. 'Yes! Yes! That's the place! Hurry, man!'

But before Jeff's fingers could clutch the bag, Micky breathed, 'Look!' with such intensity that they all moved, standing close together, staring across the road.

For desperate seconds Martha could see nothing behind the glare of the Range Rover. Then things glittered in the moonlight, tips of objects in a circle, objects, she realised, too hot to retain their caps of snow.

'The King's men!' whispered the doctor.

'The Rollright Stones!' breathed Martha. Then her shoulders hunched with fear. 'Oh, God!' she said, and the three men stepped in front of her and Mummy. 'Oh, God help us! Send Daddy! Send Daddy!' for the thing that walked like a man rose darkly from behind the far hedgerow; tall, jaws glinting; and across the countryside fell a cry, thin and distant, full of longing and wickedness.

In a single leap the beast cleared the hedge and crouched on the snowy road.

'If I can get behind it—' said Jeff.

104

Micky snapped the shotgun closed. 'Get the girls into the car,' he told his father, but Jeff's mighty arm reached out and the shotgun changed hands.

'Get the girls into the car,' murmured Jeff.

Micky bent swiftly and lifted the shovel. He nudged the little doctor aside. 'Get the girls into the car.' And even in that terrible moment as the creature loped closer, those brave words amused Martha; then the doctor started to obey, leaving Micky and Jeff shoulder to shoulder, with no barrier but the straggling hedge between them and their dreadful enemy.

'Come.' Dr Bellamy looked around, then hesitated. There was no way they could get to the Range Rover.

Very calmly he gazed at Martha, then Mummy. 'I'm sorry,' he said. 'I have a feeling I started all this by digging here.' He removed his anorak and put it around Mummy who was shivering in her dress. Then he became a third warrior, a magnificent gnome beside the dark bulk of Jefferson Wilson and the lesser outline of his son.

Martha closed her eyes as the creature paused. She forced her thoughts to the front of her brain. She said, 'Daddy,' inside her head.

Mummy's arms enclosed her and from the doctor's anorak rose the sweet smell of pipe tobacco. Martha didn't move. There was so little time. 'Daddy,' she called into the infinite silence of her mind. 'Hurry, Daddy.'

'It seems unsure,' muttered the doctor.

'*Daddy!*'

'Our shots earlier don't seem to have wounded it,' whispered Jeff.

A great silence filled the world. The snuffling beyond the hedge was suddenly unimportant. Martha felt that love reigned between the stars, that cosmic wisdom bound the universe in ultimate joy. She remembered deciding before that fear existed only within her; now joy poured through her heart and her brain radiated with light—

'It's going to pounce!' gasped Micky.

Mummy's arms squeezed Martha from her trance.

'There's someone coming!'

The headlights of the Range Rover cut a brilliant corridor across the road. The Rollright Stones shone dimly with moonlight. The creature behind the hedge turned away, pacing nervously, close to the beam.

Beyond the light, strode a man, a shadow among shadows, dark movement in darkness. He stopped, unseen behind the glare.

'Get away!' croaked Jeff. 'Get into the car!'

The figure didn't move.

Warmth engulfed Martha.

The stars sang.

The world was a glittering white jewel.

'It's Daddy,' she said simply.

The creature leapt.

Not towards Micky and Jeff and the little doctor, but towards the shape beyond the light. It leapt savagely, more wolf than man. Snowflakes fell lazily. It became a black bulk with the beam behind it. The figure opened its arms as if in welcome, and the werewolf twisted desperately as if seeing a creature more dreadful than itself, but it couldn't stop.

It dropped into the man's embrace, and the shriek that fell across the frozen countryside curdled Martha's heart, and the moonglow faded and snowflakes spun into the light.

The figures dissolved.

'Daddy!' screamed Martha. She ripped herself from

Mummy and dashed through the hedge into the dazzling headlights.

'Daddy?' she moaned.

She turned round and round, weeping, searching.

'Daddy!'

She sat in the snow.

There was no one.

Chapter 11

She slept in the Range Rover.

It stopped, and she stumbled out to stand bewildered under the lamp-post at the cottage. Snow lay thick.

Jeff walked into the trees. Martha understood. Angus was coming home.

She wept hopelessly as Mummy and Dr Bellamy guided her to the kitchen door. Micky went past the door towards the garden; and inside, as she slumped on the settee shuddering with cold, she heard a spade strike soil. Micky, gravedigger.

The doctor stared at her over his beard, kindly eyes, a glass; she drank and bitter strength swept her throat. He seemed unaffected by the cold and the terror. Daddy's good friend. And now theirs.

Mummy packed wood and coal into the stove. She drank her brandy. Her face was white.

The spade cut the earth, the sound cut the night.

Noises faded around Martha. Heat from the stove touched her eyelids. The glass slid from her fingers.

The library was warm.

Martha, in her nightdress, curled herself into the darkness of an armchair and watched the embers in the fireplace. The other fire, beyond the curtained window, flared and shadows danced in gleeful silence across the many rows of books.

She closed her scrap book of pressed leaves and laid it aside. She caressed the shiny surface of her book on plants, and smiled. The weeping was over. Daddy and Angus were beloved memories, the pain of their loss dulled in a few short weeks.

Earlier that day Martha and Mummy had prepared a special meal. The silver had left Martha's fingers black after an hour of polishing spoons and forks, knives and salad servers; leaving the metal white and perfectly shining.

Jeff and Micky had arrived exactly at seven, both looking strong and handsome in their best clothes; both smelling of aftershave.

They had talked little of their strange adventure, for talk too, was in the past, but Martha knew that the fragments of the shaman's stone were harmless, safe with Dr Bellamy, merely cold and interesting after the creature vanished. She smiled again at the embers, turning her silver pencil with the 2B lead in her fingers. Dr Bellamy was distressing the vicar with demands to cut the largest fragment from the church wall.

Perhaps the doctor, or someone like him, would solve the riddle of the standing stones. Or perhaps some clergyman or mystic, sensitive to the deepest rhythms of life, would open a door to this secret knowledge. Martha turned her thoughts away from the vicar with his false glances and quivering fear.

She lifted her two volumes, went to her desk, and put the books in a drawer. Beside Daddy's picture of Stonehenge was a photograph of Angus, his great head tilted enquiringly at the camera. Behind him, a pair of legs went up into the frame. At dinner, when Jeff had given her the photograph there was merry argument about whose legs they were, both Micky and Jeff denying their feet were that big. And Mummy had laughed.

Mummy was happy now. The adventure had left something very precious. The knowledge that Daddy, though dead in this world, was alive; and, thought Martha, Angus is alive too, perhaps with Daddy, walking beside him through a different landscape.

She touched the photograph with her knuckle.

Then she lifted her pad from the desk and curled again in the armchair. Jeff and Micky had gone home. Mummy was asleep upstairs.

By the glow of the fires she peered at the first blank page of her pad.

She put the tip of the silver pencil to the paper.

She began to write.

Author's note

Readers interested in standing stones should try Francis Hitching's lovely book *Earth Magic* published by Cassell. It tells of energy spiralling around many ancient stones; and the strange story of a lady dowser at Rollright who dropped her pendulum—a length of thread with a weight on the end—into the tall grass. She found it, with the thread standing rigid, and so firm she could scarcely bend it.

Hugh Scott